Depression Kids

One Family's Season of Life

By Wade Hampton Kinsey Jr.

Depression Kids — One Family's Season of Life

First Edition — Laurel Ridge Publisher

Printed in the United States of America
by Multi Business Press

Library of Congress Catalog Number: 95-077025

ISBN 0-927562-17-0

Pictured on the cover are author Wade Hampton Kinsey, Jr. and older brother Frank Robb Kinsey—circa 1922

The author formerly published

After All

This personal account of experiences in an infantry company in Italy during W.W. II contains graphic descriptions of combat, Italian customs, poetry, pictures, and heartfelt reaction. It is available from Drummer Boy Books, 119 S. Market Street, Ligonier, PA, 15658. $9.95, tax to PA addresses, $2.00 P&H.

Depression Kids

can also be obtained from
Drummer Boy Books, 119 S. Market Street
Ligonier, PA 15658
$10.95, tax to PA addresses, $2.00 P&H

Also obtained from Partnership Book Services
135 North Main, Hillsboro, KS 67063

Acknowledgements

— To God, who makes all things possible.

Accolades are due to my wife, Pauline "Polly" Kinsey, whose untiring confidence, urging, optimism, and patience during the effort to begin and sustain this work deserve much credit. Her countless hours of typing from almost illegible handwriting attest to her determination.

Rev. Hugh Stouppe, a long time pastor, friend, and mentor, lent encouragement at every turn and freely gave the benefit of his experience. Everyone should be so fortunate as to have such a cherished companion.

Walter Jaap inspired me to write about parental influence, the awareness of which may be beneficial to present and future generations.

Jean Kuhn suggested changing a previously considered title.

Joe Newman brought to my attention some superfluous wordage.

Betty Jo Cairns patiently transcribed to electron discs and proofed copies. She also corrected many of the author's errors.

Bruce A. Hess generously gave of his time for proof reading.

Many of my parents' descendants offered enthusiastic encouragement. It is the fond hope of the writer that they as equally approve the results.

The writing for this book was completed and put on tape in late summer of 1994. Almost immediately thereafter, the Author was informed that he had contracted a terminal illness and would not be capable of bringing the book to print. A niece, Wanda Kinsey Hess insisted this could and should be done without further concern on the part of the author. She had long encouraged and hoped that the story be recorded for her progeny and that of other relatives, and for the interest, knowledge and benefit of following generations of young Americans. With encouragement and assistance from other nieces and nephews, she endeavored to bring this book to print and distribution. It is hoped that none of the well wishers will suffer disappointment or loss in this endeavor.

Having been poor is no shame,
but being ashamed of it is.

B. Franklin

Dedication

This writing is respectfully dedicated to the memory of my parents and to all the devoted parents of the era. Their faithfulness and examples for future generations have not yet been fully appreciated.

Preface

There are three rules for writing a novel.
Unfortunately no one knows what they are.

W. Somerset Maugham

The above, I presume, could apply to any sort of expression. Although the subject here treated could have many sources and applications, it was intended to be confined to a certain era and place. It was my lot to be the last surviving male of a large family. As is probably a general occurrence, the children of siblings approach survivors seeking information relative to the early lives of their parents, insisting that some history be recorded. Although there may be some other defense for writing yet another book for an already overcrowded market, the above would have been the principal influence.

Some other people, not directly related, have insisted it would be a boon to this and future generations to be aware of the hardships endured by their ancestors. Furthermore, it is suggested that all of society should be more grateful for blessings which have always been taken for granted. Thirdly, when one engages in conversation with anyone who refers to himself or herself as having been a "depression kid," they seem to show somewhat of a sense of pride and accomplishment in having survived.

Some people have gone so far as to say "What this country needs is another depression." While this is a radical idea, the period certainly gave rise to some qualities that more recently have vanished as far as this writer is concerned. Even in the pre-depression era a great deal of frugality had to be practiced. The "great depression" is described as beginning with the stock market crash in October, 1929, and continuing through the 1930's.

Consider some things brought to public attention in 1921 when the author was five years old.

Warren Harding was the 29th President. The unknown soldier was buried in Arlington Cemetery. Two-ton Pierce-Arrow trucks sold for $3750. A song about "April Showers" was released. A Brer Rabbit cookbook was available. "President" suspenders sold for fifty cents. A new car could be bought for about $400. However, a Dort sedan listed at about $1100. Gasoline was about eleven cents per gallon. Car radios appeared. Champion spark plugs cost seventy-five cents each. Asbestos roofing was available. Deluxe "ice boxes" were touted. Milk was about fifty cents per gallon. Life expectancy was fifty-four years.

Since the author was born in 1916, reference will be made to happenings from that time and into what is thought of as the recovery.

There is no intent to be exclusive. Should anyone, not related by blood lines or not having lived through the Depression, wish to be apprised or reminded of the era, read on.

Table of Contents

CHAPTER 1

Community

This writing relates to a village located between Laurel Mountain and Chestnut Ridge in Western Pennsylvania, a village called Waterford. When references are made to the mountain, they mean Laurel Hill. A trout stream called Mill Creek runs through; it gathered its flow from three fresh water tributaries in the mountain and several farm land feeders. There were probably forty-five houses in the village, and numerous farms and single houses scattered over the school district. The Menoher highway ran the length of it, and four roads led in from the farm areas.

The time frame for this writing ran approximately from 1916 to 1938 overlapping, at times, on both ends. Some things are difficult to date from memory. All the time, however, would be considered to be during the depression, even before the stock market crash in 1929.

In the early part of this period, there was no electricity and no running water until Works Progress Administration Projects in the 1930's. At this writing, there is still no natural gas, although it was available four miles away at Ligonier. The running water came about because the village had the highest typhoid fever rate in Pennsylvania.

The village lies on bottom land, which was very porous and contained rounded creek stones which had rolled down the changing stream for centuries. Underground rivulets were numerous. Also, all families had outdoor toilets, and eventually drainage from them seeped into the wells. Delegations of citizens, doctors, attorneys, and lawmakers motored to Washington

D.C. appealing for help. I'm not aware if, or how much, the citizens were required to contribute. In any event, governmental aid made possible a small reservoir and distribution system in the 1930's. In due time outdoor toilets diminished and all but disappeared. This meant that each household had its own septic system, as there was no sewer or treatment plant.

Much of what will be written will pre-date both the water system and electricity. This will show to best advantage the many conveniences we all now enjoy and, incidentally, appreciate too little. Anyone who takes the time to read it may find a joy of some new insight in the reading. Perhaps they will relive some old experience and may find a greater gratitude for today's blessings.

Life here was lived on a very personal level. No strangers lived here because all were known to each other. Indeed, even a dog on the loose could be identified with its proper family. There were few automobiles and only a couple families had telephones. There was no public transportation, and radios were non-existent. It was almost a self-centered little world.

There was an organization known as "The Literary Society" which existed strictly for the purpose of entertaining. Some enjoyed participating; a few came only to observe. The meetings were held in the schoolhouse when it was a two-room layout. All seats would be occupied and all aisles filled with standing observers. Lighting was provided by wall-hung kerosene lamps. Programming was varied and included such things as readings, reciting poetry, singing and playing instrumental music. Debates, mock court trials, boxing exhibitions, story telling, jokes, blackboard drawing, short plays, and extemporaneous speaking were also included. They would select a number of speakers and assign the topic a couple of minutes before the speech was to begin.

On one instance, a local farm boy had returned from a visit to a farm in the West. His subject was to "discuss farming in the West." His speech—"Farming in the West is like farming in the East; it's a failure." He sat down to a rousing ovation.

On another occasion, a man who had played the part of a

powdered, gray-headed man was, in short time, teamed in a boxing exhibition. When he received a sharp blow to the head, a cloud of powder rose from his hair. The audience found this quite humorous.

When I was still a preschooler, someone presented a harmonica to me. Though I learned to play a discernible tune, I was shy and did not wish to become a public spectacle. My Dad, however, offered to give me a nickel. That was a great deal more money than it has ever been since.

It would be wonderful to have remembered more of the activities. I do recall that my first impression of a court trial was gained by observing a mock trial where my heavier built Uncle Cicero, the cobbler, acted as judge.

All in all, the Society was a blessing to residents who had precious little entertainment or humor in their lives. As stated elsewhere, the churches allowed for a great deal of interchange, but one met the same members repeatedly. In the Society there was the opportunity to meet folks outside of your church circle.

There may have been other barbers in town, but I went to Bill Knupp's home where his barber chair was kept in the corner of his living room. When someone came for a haircut, he would lift the chair out of the corner, throw a cover over the customer's body, and trim the hair with hand-operated clippers. If his hand moved too fast and the clippers were not operating fast enough, a small patch of hair would be pulled out, leaving a white spot known as a "cat step." This was painful but endurable; and anyway, there was no choice in the matter. His house abutted our lot, and he charged only fifteen cents for a haircut.

He was a very versatile and hard-working man. He repaired clocks and shoes, wove rugs, rented and kept a truck patch, and worked as a stonemason. He also was a faithful member of the Christian Church where he was a teacher and elder. His family consisted of four boys and one girl. He was a man of even temper and clean language. I never knew of him having a confrontation with anyone. He was deserving of a great deal of respect.

The men in the community who had been long-time friends

enjoyed a mutual trust. If one of them fell upon hard times, he could go to a friend and borrow a sum of money to alleviate a minor emergency. No thought was given to legalities. The contract was a handshake, and repayment would be made as early as practical.

There were several classes of itinerants who appeared, mostly in warm weather. Barney Wolfe was one of these. He came with a gray-white horse which pulled his covered wagon. I seem to remember that he sold clothes for adults and children alike. There would be pots, pans, cutlery, knick-knacks, and blankets. Sometimes he had chairs, both rockers and straight, hanging on the side of the wagon. He would not necessarily have the same items each time he came. It would appear that he bought whatever he could find that had the probability of selling or he had the opportunity to acquire at his sources. I never knew where his home base was, but it must have been a distance away as he came only a few times each summer.

Joe Richey had a fruit market in Ligonier and also peddled his wares from a truck out in the valley. A scale hung over the tailgate for weighing produce. I was never to know how he kept it, but he usually had ice cream packed in some sort of cabinet. He sold it by the cone while children who could scrape up a nickel awaited anxiously. Not too long ago I heard the rumor from an old timer that he also had a cache of moonshine somewhere out of sight on his truck.

Abie Marks, who also lived in Ligonier, was known as the "junk man" as he bought any kind of metal, be it old farm machinery, broken tools, parts of angle iron—anything metal. Some of the lads who roamed into the mountain, where an old railroad from lumbering days had deteriorated, carried back all manner of booty. This might include old crosscut saws, broken axes, railroad spikes, or odd pieces not identified. Abie also bought old rubber items, including rarely found tires.

Periodically, a man came along carrying a one-legged stand by a strap over his shoulder. Attached to it was a small hand grinder with which he sharpened knives, scissors, and small tools. He also riveted holes in buckets or pots. He had some bows for repairing umbrellas and would make other tinkering repairs of an odd nature.

Although they usually passed through in one day, there were quite a few tramps or bums, as they were referred to by the locals. When they asked for food, Mom would never turn them away hungry, but would serve whatever happened to be available among left-overs or sandwiches. We always heard that they had a way of marking a house where one could get a hand out.

Against this background, let us think about very personal family life and times.

Honor Thy Father and Mother

Exodus 20:12

Mother, LaOphia   Father, Wade Sr.

CHAPTER 2

Mom

Many songs, poems, and accolades have been appropriately recorded about mothers, and quite rightfully so. Almost all people show reverence, devotion, and love for their mothers—a few exceptions noted. Once when a lady (Roberta Naugle Schwarz), who had been reared only a short distance from our home, visited my sister, Estella Thomas, she remarked that someone should write a book about our Mom. At the time no one took the remark seriously, as writing a book was something most people never attempted. As for me, I could never feel that justice could be done. This does not reflect on her unselfish devotion to family, but on my ability to give sufficient credit to such a life of devotion. Though I still do not feel qualified to do so, it would seem unlikely that anything could be written about the era without reference to her contribution. Where to begin?

Presumably, it would be proper to express gratitude to her memory and to the Providence which positioned her at this time and place. It would be hard to imagine her contribution having been made by any lesser person. She could not possibly loom larger than she stands in the memories of all who knew her. Having stated this, it now becomes even more difficult to characterize her day-to-day existence. It is likely she was taken somewhat for granted, as seems a typical human trait.

The observation of the aforementioned lady visitor was, of course, made from a distance. She had seen Mom from outside the family life and only on an occasional basis. It was, however, the attitude of all who knew Mom. In addition to her faithfulness at home, she was very helpful to anyone in distress of any sort. This would include mid-wifery to women in the neighborhood, lunch for an itinerant person, or some sort of community service. Though it was obvious she had plenty to do at home, there was time for quilting for the church circle and teaching in Sunday school or in a teacher's training course. The very efficient way she accomplished duties at home was crowned by her affable disposition. That she refrained from saying anything detrimental to another was not the result of some platitude or old saw: it was a part of her philosophy and practice. Furthermore, in spite of difficulties in her own life, she tried to instill faith and optimism in the family. She once told me that one could never get into serious trouble by telling the truth. Although she had precious little time for personal diversion, she dearly loved to read; and indeed, by this practice, she became essentially a self-made and knowledgeable person. She enjoyed doing crossword puzzles and was very conversant in matters of Scripture. Her library was very limited for lack of both space and affluence. She did have a few Gene Stratton Porter books and a small cardboard display case containing little leather-bound books, such as Evangeline and similar popular volumes. She read periodicals as she could find time and borrowed books when possible. As I grew older, I was amazed to assess the breadth of her knowledge for one with only a "common school" education.

Like most mothers of the day, she "wore many hats." She was most proficient in the kitchen and, by today's standards, had very little with which to work. It would take a great deal of imagination for current housewives to realize the difficulty of operating without electricity, running water, or natural gas, and all the added burdens of these absences. Elsewhere references are made to the bother and extra work.

Perhaps it is time to say that she lived through fourteen pregnancies and the death of five of the resulting children. There were many large families in that era and few families of two or three children. I have always considered myself fortunate in having been born into a large family, perhaps because I was at the latter end of it. In honesty, it must be recognized that as the family size diminished, Mom would have had more time to spend with me; but there was never any evidence that she showed partiality. When the number dwindled to one, of course, that one got all the attention. Naturally, at my own insistence, there was never any thought of my being spoiled! Of course there was a lot of assistance, guidance, and protection, from siblings and parents alike. Children in smaller families would have more of clothing, toys, and perhaps other things not considered; none-the-less, the closeness, concern, companionship, and perhaps some rivalry were very rewarding; and except in rare instance, few "clutch" children would wish to trade places.

She must have agonized much over the illness of a child. In those days doctoring was principally a homegrown practice. The nearest doctors were four long miles away and, for financial reasons, were called only in the most severe circumstances. In the event of contagious diseases, the unaffected children would be "farmed out" to a relative or neighbor for the duration. Traditional and home cures were the general solution. Though I never remembered it, when very small I climbed up on a chair and stuck my finger in hot jelly on the stove. I was taken to Granny Beam who "took the fire out" by some traditional method which I don't recall. I still have ten fingers.

I do recall that Mom had the most tender touch. Her hands on a fevered brow seemed to work magic. If she rubbed "Vicks" salve on a chest and back, relief was almost certain. I distinctly remember the shape of her hands, particularly the thumbs. She could wrap a cut finger (Band-Aids were nonexistent) with some treatment such as peroxide and a salve which could have been homemade Balm-of-Gilead, White Cloverline, Rose Bud, or Porter's Pain King. Porter also made a liniment which was used.

Sometimes during my latter preschool years I would get bored and remember saying "What can I do now?" Mom would suggest some amusement such as coloring with crayons, leafing through a picture book, cracking hickory nuts, shelling field corn, paring potatoes for supper, or even reading to me. She always had answers.

She once remarked that she liked to work. What a blessing, in as much as there was so much of it to be done! When cooking didn't occupy all of her time, especially in summer, she liked to work in the garden and always had an interest in her flower beds. She would go with us to the potato patch when there was hoeing to be done. In season she would go with a group for berry picking, usually huckleberries, which would have to be carried three miles home. By the next day they needed to be canned in glass jars with screw-top lids.

Referring to the community service mentioned earlier, I recall that as a small boy I would accompany her to the home of Mrs. Etta Cramp where the ladies of the church would have a quilt in frames, and would gather on certain evenings to quilt or piece a new one as the situation demanded.

Proceeds from the sale of the quilts would be directed to whatever project was presently being planned. Often this could be used for furnishing needed supplies for Sunday school, a church-wide need, or foreign missionary work.

Perhaps a quilting bee is best recalled by me for an unrelated aspect. In summer we would go immediately after supper, I in bare feet. Since the conversation was of no great interest to me, I would often fall asleep on the floor. Upon leaving I would be partially aroused to go home in the dark, stubbing a toe on some protruding stone, sobbing, and hobbling on. When we arrived home, the washing session always included the feet—a most distasteful chore for a tired and sleepy lad. An old song line said "Memories are made of things like this."

Mom was reared in a one-parent family. Though she obviously had a caring mother, her father was never a part of her life. She did have caring uncles, aunts, and grandparents. By current standards she could possibly have made this lack in her life an alibi for some imagined shortfall, looked for a scapegoat, and become embittered. Instead, she simply accepted the reality and saw to it that there was no neglect in her devotion to her own family.

There must have been times when the burdens of rearing a large family became exceedingly heavy. I feel with all my being, however, that it never crossed the minds of either of our parents to "cut and run," as has been done by so many parents of recent years. They were in marriage for the long haul—"until death do us part."

If you would permit a momentary glance through a time tunnel, it may be good to relate a part of a conversation with a "depression kid" as we spoke recently at a men's breakfast. We were dwelling on the subject of children in those days eating whatever was served. The speaker did not especially like soup, which his mother served often. One day he noticed that she was not eating soup, which he was obliged to eat. Not until much later did he realize that the soup may have been in short supply, and she refrained so there would be more for the children. This is a typical mother's sacrifice.

Since we have just glanced through a time tunnel, this may be an appropriate time to relate an incident from Mom's later life. During a visit to her when she was on her death bed, I would read one of her favorite scriptures. Once she chose the Twelfth Chapter of Romans. As I came to the seventeenth verse, she interrupted me to dwell on the thought which read "Recompense to no man evil for evil." Finally she said, "That's a pretty good rule to live by." We then finished the chapter.

I recall hearing her say that she hoped she could leave the world a better place than she had found it. Without fear of contradiction, I can state emphatically that she did!

Echoes

Though years have gone since Mother passed
Still speaks she many times to me
Of tenets taught in ways, the best
For childhood eyes to vaguely see

In books depicting ways of life,
With honor and with peace of mind
And Oh! the pattern of herself
Impressed the thoughtless to be kind

With clippings of some forceful verse
That spoke about another goal
"Spare something of your meager purse,
Buy hyacinths to feed the soul."

When patience is in short supply
And danger looms of temper lost
I look out through my memory's eye
And hear her murmur, "Count the cost."

In answer to a soldier's quest
About the psalmist who he reads
Returns the answer briefest, best
And hope, to fill an urgent need.

In hymn and scripture come again
The things she stressed in early days
Standing in accents bright and plain,
Her voice is heard in curious ways.

Oh! Could more mothers such as she
Be present in our land today
To help the little children see
The truths of God along their way.

Unworthy, may I still come home
To find her waiting at the door,
Thy mercy having penned my name,
And take her in my arms once more.

W.K. 1986
Sainted Mother, help me to acquire your
concern, love, and giving which made of
you such a blessed example.

Mother's Gift

I've seen flowers at grand exhibitions
In classes, divisions, and sorts
And folks came for miles to behold them
And all of their beauty report.

I've seen flowers at banquets and weddings
There were roses, gardenias, and glads
And corsages on long evening dresses
All colors, shapes, sizes, and fads.

I've seen them in flower shop windows
As into the shop I would delve
"These roses," he'd say, "are a bargain:
they're only three fifty for twelve."

But the ones that I really enjoy
Like zinnia, cock's comb, marigold
With scarlet sage, dahlia, and aster
Are given to me and not sold.

The reason I treasure them highly
Is not for the price, you will see
But for love of them gently instilled
By a wonderful mother, in me.

W.K.

Mom and Dad

Family portrait with the ten children.

CHAPTER 3

Dad

Having been born in 1874, my father was forty-two years old when I was born. He was a spare fellow of about six feet in height with large hands and long legs. For much of his life he had a mustache. His weight was a matter of guesswork, but suffice to say he carried no excess flesh. He was a meticulous person who did not believe in doing things by the halves—unnecessarily so, we children sometimes felt. He was fiercely independent so far as the outside world was concerned and a strict disciplinarian at home. For right or wrong, his German ancestry always bore a great deal of credit for this. He was a fourth generation American of German extraction, and the family name was originally spelled Kintzy at the time of emigration. He was somewhat of an enigma, being both firm and kind. He had the innate capacity for making things happen, rather than letting them happen.

By trade, he was a stonemason at which he generally worked in summers. For the most part this would cease in cold weather when mortar would freeze before it could set. In winter he sometimes worked in coal mines in the area. During one such time he had the audacity to join the miner's union. Coal and iron police would sometimes arrive as strike breakers, and one could find his head in his hand if the situation got critical. One of his brothers assured him that he would never again be able to get a job. As it developed, his action did not hinder him from getting work elsewhere. In the early days unions were not as well coordinated as they later became.

I have no way of knowing how many winters he took this

course, but some of the winters he worked for an ice company which had a pond about five miles from home. Winters were severe, and ice formed to a thickness to support laborers and even the teams of horses used in scoring the ice. When a cube of ice was broken away from the mass, it would be divided into manageable sizes and loaded on railroad cars adjacent to the pond. It was hauled to Pittsburgh, and probably other cities, where it would be insulated with sawdust and kept until summer. There was also an ice house across from our home, but it was out of operation before my time. In any event, Dad walked five miles to the "Ice Pond," worked ten hours, and then walked home. He was never home in daylight for a greater part of the winter.

There was logging in progress part way through the century, and some winters he would work in the woods. Men would be employed to wield cross-cut saws and axes to fell and trim trees for feeding sawmills where, again, there was heavy labor to be performed. There were few easy jobs in those days, and workers toiled long hours.

Work at his trade naturally paid more money, and he would be sought after. Just about the time that I was old enough to remember, he worked at his trade in building the Rolling Rock Clubhouse above Laughlintown. This was a sizable undertaking; and most of the available masons in the area, along with some imports, were engaged. They worked nine hours a day and on a cloudless week could work fifty-four hours, which Dad called a "ringer", at one dollar per hour—fifty-four dollars for the week! The sandpaper effect of the stone wore away the skin of the fingers. I remember seeing his skin worn through the epidermis and little spots of blood from capillaries showing. He would massage them with some variety of salve at night and return to work the next day. I don't recall him ever wearing gloves for stone work, nor could I suggest a reason for this.

Apparently, higher wages were being paid elsewhere. One day one of the officers of the Club was viewing the work; and Dad, egged on by the other masons, approached him relative to an increase of pay on this job. The reply was to the effect that the member felt a dollar per hour was adequate for "country" masonry. Whereupon Dad, seeing no difference between country and city masonry, became incensed, gathered his tools, and left the job. He always insisted that he never left a job but that he found another. His reputation as a mason or laborer was established.

As children growing into young adulthood, we would sometimes be hired for some sort of services that we were capable of performing. Dad always admonished us, boy or girl, that if we were going to take an employer's money, we should give a day's work for a day's pay.

It is evident that in the past most people used formulae they did not comprehend. They simply knew that, by tradition, they worked. For example, when Dad squared a foundation, he used a 6,8,10 formula. He knew that by marking along the lines six feet from the corner on one side and eight feet on the other, if the marks were ten feet apart, the foundation would be square arriving at the point of origin. We boys did not know why it worked until high school geometry showed us. Geometry taught that the square of the length of the arms of a right-angle triangle equals the square of the hypotenuse—the distance between the marks on the line (6x6=36, 8x8=64, =100 - 10x10=100).

Doubtless, many recipes and medication formulae had scientific reasons not known to the users—suffice to say they worked.

As a result of being hit in the eye with a spall while trimming stone, Dad was blinded in the right eye. He was disturbed when people approached on the "blind side" without his knowledge. In the present day, his blindness could probably have been prevented.

He was never troublesome and wished always to get on with neighbors and friends. If accosted, however, he never ran from a fight. An incident which took place before my time became an oft told tale in the village. On the mountain above the village lived a family of known rogues. Three of the boys traveled in a sort of pack and terrorized peace loving citizens. One of them would pick a fight; if he were being beaten, the other two would join in. On one occasion the brother whose first name was Keen apparently picked on Dad in front of a crowd of locals. As the struggle went on, the brothers edged in to interfere. The locals, however, came forward to restrain them saying in effect "this one is going to be fair." In the melee, Dad was bitten through the lower lip but was gaining advantage; whereupon the fight ceased, and the rogues retreated to the mountain. Keen threatened revenge, which concern persisted for some time in the locale. Later, Dad was walking a trail with a small son perched on his shoulder. He saw Keen at a distance, and no trouble ensued. He felt the incident had ended, which apparently it had.

The rogues apparently carried out their depredations elsewhere. It recently became known that they had a degree of refinement. They loved to sing and did it rather well. One of them also played the organ and, on good behavior, were reported to have been well met.

Much later, I shaved Dad with an electric razor the last three years of his life. The scar on his lip was still discernible but had grown dim. It was the means of my hearing about the episode.

Secondary activities in which he was variously engaged included a keen interest in The Pittsburgh Post and the Democratic Party. He served on the board of the local cemetery company, voted faithfully, served for a term as constable, and held memberships in sportsmen's clubs, etc. In 1923 he instigated a family reunion of his father's descendants. It grew to include cousins and second cousins until it has a membership of thousands scattered throughout the land today. Two family histories have been written, and a third one is in the making.

He was known locally for his first-aid work for which he had no training except observation and experience. Let us think about a few of the incidents. One night a man who was married to one of Dad's nieces came to his door having been beaten by his brother-in-law. He was reported as being a bloody mess of bruises, black eyes, and lacerations. He would have been treated with the limited medication available. Clell Kissell, a fellow stonemason and outdoorsman, came insisting to have an aching tooth pulled. This was accomplished by use of pliers and continued rinse of warm salt water. My sister, Estella, had a broken forearm sustained from a fall from the old apple tree. He set and splinted the break which healed without incident. His son, Glenn, jumped a fence and landed on a broken bottle causing a large gash across the arch of his foot. The injured sat on the front steps while his sister, Myrtle, carried basins of cold water from the well near which sat Dad reading a newspaper. The bleeding continued till Myrtle lost her nerve and informed Dad. Seeing the injury, he sent Myrtle for Crystal Luther, a neighbor and practical nurse. Together they cleaned and sewed the gash with a flesh needle and bandaged it. The flesh needle leads to another incident. A man attempted, but failed, suicide. He cut his throat, but not successfully. When a doctor arrived, he needed help to restrain the fellow and called Dad for help. The victim remonstrated against the pain, and the doctor said "You started this and Kinsey and I are going to finish it." They did, after which the doctor gave his helper the flesh needle.

During recess at school, Wade Jr., who was by then in the "upper" room, fell against a seat across the aisle and cut his forehead horizontally for a generous inch. The teacher was frightened, sent for Dad, and offered to take us to the doctor. She was assured that the cut could be treated at home where the head was laid back on the table and the wound cleaned with peroxide. A court plaster (a cotton strip with adhesive on one side) was placed on both sides of the cut. They were then drawn together and held by butterfly patches of the same material. The scar was less obvious than if it had been sewn.

His ministrations were not confined to the human race. People who had male piglets to be castrated sent for Dad. He would slit the skin in two places with a sharp point pocket knife, squeeze out the testicles, and sever the cords. This was usually followed by rubbing the area generously with lard and releasing the piglet. The operation required assistance, usually performed by his younger sons if the owner was not available. No charge was made.

In another instance, the pastor of our church, a part-time farmer, kept registered Jersey cows. One of them fell down a steep bank and broke a hind leg. The preacher felt the cow had to be destroyed and offered her to Dad. Dad was confident that if the leg could be splinted, the bone would knit. A funeral director/furniture dealer was making a furniture delivery and offered the use of his truck, a long-bed, black Dodge without dual wheels. Somehow, the cow was cradled in a belt/chain apparatus which was fastened to the joint above the cow stall in the stable. The leg was splinted and indeed did knit, after which she walked naturally. I don't know how long the poor thing stood and hung there, but she had to be restrained. After she healed, the pastor tried to buy her back, but she was not for sale. Nor do I know how many years she helped to support a large family. She was affectionately called "Fawn."

In yet another incident which happened later in my life, my older brother, Alfred, owned a general store in the village. He bought and sold large tubes of bologna which were tied at the end with a rope for hanging. He had a family dog, mostly terrier, whose name was "Billy." Billy found an end cut of bologna which was still attached to one of the ropes. In eating the end cut he also ate the rope, which lodged after only beginning to emerge at the dog's rear end. Dad was called upon to bring about relief to the poor animal. He administered an enema with generous amount of very soapy water and set Billy on the road to health again.

Sometimes a cow suffered from constipation, usually the result of eating too much or the wrong kind of fodder. Dad would administer treatment by use of a very long-necked bottle filled with a heavy solution of epsom salts in water. The head of the cow would be raised, the long neck of the bottle inserted between the cheek and gum while the throat was being stroked to induce swallowing. This process was called drenching.

We once had a cow which broke out of a pasture into a corn field and over-indulged in the green juicy leaves. Before this could be digested, it evidently produced a gas which caused much bloating and agony. This condition Dad apparently did not feel qualified to treat. He sent for John Hoffer, who owned a combination feed and grocery store. John had treated this condition in other cows by puncturing the abdomen. The trick was in knowing where to puncture. Mr. Hoffer knew, and did so, to the relief of both cow and owner.

In a later day he no doubt would have come under scrutiny for practicing without a license. His work, however, was all charity, and he likely would have been warned and exonerated of wrong doing.

It seems as though some people in the community felt Dad was an over-strict disciplinarian with his children. He was at the same time capable of some very kind and tender deeds. He had an empathy for people in distress, and offered such assistance as he was able. As was the practice in the village, when a death occurred, he and others would dig and cover graves without thought of compensation.

He had an elder sister, Margaret, who lived on the edge of the village. It had been the practice in the family to preface the name of siblings with the title "Brother" or "Sister." Often on a Sunday afternoon he would go to visit "Sister Mag." She was a slight little lady, the mother of numerous grown children. As was common, she smoked a clay pipe which she carried in an apron pocket. Dad often took paper of "cut and dry" tobacco for her—not that it was so highly valued, but it was a gesture of love and concern; and I could imagine them smoking their pipes together under a grape or rose arbor. Often he would bring a few sweet smelling buds from her shrub bush for Mom. The odor would be enhanced if the buds were held in the hand.

When Frank and I were in high school ('29 to '33), we spent some of our Christmas vacations working in the woods with Dad. He had decided to establish a retirement fund in the form of a new loghouse. He was employed by a man who owned a country estate and who, when he found that Dad could hew logs, decided to build an addition to an existing loghouse. A deal was made whereby after the completion of the addition, Dad could have logs for his new house from the employer's stand of timber. We helped to fell the trees with an axe and a cross-cut saw. A part of the tree top was left intact to prevent the log from turning while being hewn with a broad axe. Dad had learned to hew earlier in life, although little of it was being done at this time in history.

When the foundation and deck were built for the new house, he erected a pole in the deck center. It was higher than the desired height of the top logs and had a metal ring on the top which was guyed, at a distance, on four sides. A pulley was added beneath the ring, and a windlass with a crank on either side was attached to the bottom of the pole. A cantilever beam was attached and braced to the pole. It reached to the other walls of the foundation. Thus, with a second pulley on the beam, a log could be lifted from the ground and the entire rig turned to the desired wall where the log was lowered in place and notched to fit the log beneath.

Though there were many other operations involved in finish-. ing the house, these were the basic ones. The house was first

The Log House built by Dad and Sons.

rented and later sold, with the proceeds added to the retirement fund. Ironically, inflation and longevity depleted the fund; the children were able to augment his social security before his death. Both he and Mom wanted to live out their lives in their home, which they did.

There was domestic daytime help. The boys did the nursing care for Dad, the girls for Mom. During critical times, a schedule had one family member staying overnight and one staying on Sunday to relieve the domestic help. Also in the latter part of their lives, they enjoyed the comfort of automatic central heat and current appliances.

Dad probably made mistakes of which I was never aware. One I do recall was that after repeal of the 18th Amendment and the advent of the 3.2 percent beer, he opened a beer garden. The family members were not happy with the venture, and it was not lucrative enough to justify its existence. A businessman once said that if you were correct in 55% of decisions, you were a success. Dad was!

With further reference to his independent spirit, you may appreciate the story of how he chose and installed the tombstone for his wife and himself. In practicing his trade as a stonemason he was, of course, involved in all sort of stonework. On a piece of land he owned was a large egg-shaped stone which he decided to use instead of the usual marble or granite material. He dressed the bottom into a suitable surface, poured a cement base, and set the stone with the long perpendicular axis. He accomplished the move with the help of plank, rollers, bars, a half-ton pickup truck (which was backed against the corner of the higher lot), and manpower. The manpower was furnished by his son "Shupe" (Glenn) who owned the truck, son-in-law "Kelly" Thomas, and grandson George Thomas, Jr. The over-loaded truck managed to get the stone on the site, and the men managed to set it in cement on the base. Another son, Ford, acquired and had installed a bronze plate containing the data.

The family plot contains three other modest granite markers: one for our maternal grandmother, one for our fifteen-year-old sister, Jean, and one for four infants and toddlers.

Though he was a believer, during an early part of my life he did not attend church regularly as Mom and the children did. Happily, however, in his later years he not only began to attend, but was active in the church's program serving as teacher and elder. In this latter position he and Mr. Knupp (noted elsewhere) served the elements of communion. A short time before his death Dad discussed with me the approaching end. When I asked him if he were ready, he replied, "I am as ready as I'll ever be." This is the greatest comfort following the loss of a loved one. Although there were many people in that day, as in this, who performed all sorts of work on Sundays, Dad never did, except in cases of absolute necessity or emergency.

I remember Dad telling his sons, "I had a better Daddy than you will ever have"—a high compliment to my grandfather whom none of the family ever saw. He had fallen dead as he walked two miles to fill a position on the election board. He died at the age of 63.

As I wrote regarding Mom, doing justice to Dad was also not within my abilities. The longer I live, the more they are revered.

My son, hear the instruction of thy father.

Solomon
Proverbs 1:18

Like as a father pitieth his children, so the Lord pitieth them that fear him.

Psalm 103:13

CHAPTER 4

The Kitchen

The hub of activity in Mom's kitchen was the stove. Of necessity, it centered on an outside wall where the chimney was located. The chimney rose through the ceiling, attic, and peak of the roof in the one-story portion of the house. It was built of brick layers, twenty-four inches square (outside dimension). About two feet above the peak of the roof at its highest level, it was "topped out" with one row of brick overhanging slightly, presumably to have the rain drop away from its outside and away from the jointure of the brick and roof. Also, this gave it a finished appearance. On the kitchen side, and about two feet below the ceiling, a iron rung was cemented in, into which a seven-inch diameter tin stove pipe fitted. A two-inch circular flange over the pipe slid snugly against the chimney. The brick portion began about five and a half feet above the floor.

The weight of the chimney rested on vertical timbers which rested, in turn, on the floor and the cellar wall. The sides between the timbers were plastered inside and out, and the front had a head-high single board hinged with a turn snap to keep it closed. Shelves were built inside. The stove was some distance from the chimney.

The main stove top was thirty or so inches above the floor. It was about four feet long, including the covered warming tank which held about five gallons of water and was on the right hand side. The top had three removable sections each of which had two removable round lids.

Each had an indentation into which a lifter could be inserted.

The lifter had a coil handle so as not to conduct heat to the hand. This was one of the loose "tools" needed.

The top of the warming closet was about two feet above the main top; it had a nine inch shelf, and a pivoting cover on its front. It was the same length as the lid area.

The Round Oak Iron Chief Range (plain finish), Patented Contact-Plate Reservoir, and High Closet For Coal or Wood
For prices, dimensions, and weights, see page 83

Mom's stove: Round Oak Iron Chief Range
Photo courtesy of Northwestern Michigan College, Dowagiac, Michigan

The fire box which was under the left pair of lids had thin fire brick liners on the sides and back end. The bottom had a pair of grates which worked together on a cog with detachable handle through the front exterior. It was used to shake the ashes into the ash pan below. This was a rectangular metal box with a collapsible bail like a bucket and a clasp on its front. Ashes had to be removed daily. If the coal had an excessive amount of slate, the ashes would form a clinker, which sometimes needed to be removed through the lids.

It would seem likely that firing a coal range would be a simple matter of building a fire in the box and letting a natural draft up the chimney do the rest—not so! There were draft regulators below the fire box, above the fire box, and on the fixed stove pipe which went through the warming closet. There was also a damper in the pipe above the warming closet with a coiled handle outside the pipe so the damper could be set either vertically or horizontally, controlling about ninety percent of the flow. There was also a damper which operated between the stove top and oven top. It could send the flow of heat around the oven for baking or allow it to go up the pipe.

Other factors needed to be considered. Sometimes, there were variations in the quality of coal or wood used for kindling. If the air were 'heavy' or still, the pipe damper could be opened.

Periodically, soot (which is composed of carbon particles) collected. This soot acted as an insulator. It was very easily airborne and most difficult to eradicate. Disturbed, it could float over the entire kitchen and make a mess! Another tool necessary to operate a coal range was a rectangular metal piece about three inches long and three-quarters of an inch wide. This was welded, hoe-like, on one end of a thin steel rod. The opposite end was bent into a ring. This needed to be long enough to reach past all dimensions of the oven, in the spaces between the oven, in the warming tank, in the top of the oven, and underneath it. On the front of the range and below the oven door was a smaller door with a turning knob which opened into the area beneath the oven. All of the accumulated soot needed to be hooked out the small door into a container—without spilling! The hoe-like rod was hung in the flue closet. The shaker and lifter were usually kept atop the warming closet.

The stovepipe sections and elbow above the warming closet also needed cleaning periodically. They were removed, taken outside and cleaned. If they had been up a considerable time, or were showing metallic from heat, a coating of stove black was needed. Indeed, the entire stove needed to be blacked occasionally. Following soot removal, house cleaning and serious bathing was indicated.

Sometimes, when there was a soot accumulation and a roaring fire was built, the soot caught fire and flames shot out the chimney top. If the chimney was in good condition, no damage would be done except to family nerves.

Every stove needed a poker. It was used to knock down a fused topping of coal which would leave a space between the bed of hot coals and the raw coal. The poker usually had a bent ring on the handle end, or coiled steel with a space between it and the poker. If a bucket still contained coal, the poker would be stuck into it. If not, it would rest atop the warming closet on the cooking range, or on a ledge in the pot belly, or stuck into the ornamental iron work on a parlor stove.

A woodbox was in the corner of the chimney behind the left side of the range. This was needed to contain kindling at all times. The kindling had to be narrow enough to ignite from dying embers, shavings, newspapers, or dried corn cobs. It was a good season if wood had been split and neatly stacked in the low walk-in space beneath the add-on portion of the house. Otherwise, the boy, the ax, and the woodpile worked in concert to produce the desired effect. When Mom needed to kindle a fire, the necessities were on hand.

Set in the same general area were two coal buckets, the kind that slope in the front to accommodate a shovel which was kept there. It befell the lot of a boy of the right size and strength to carry the coal from the coal house.

When I was still quite small, my job description included

keeping the coal buckets full. The coal house was at the end of the walk going along the add-on portion of the house. I was not large enough or strong enough to carry two buckets full of coal simultaneously, so I filled two buckets by the coal house door. Having carried the first one to the warmth of the kitchen, I was warming my hands over the range before returning for the second bucket. Mom, on her return trip from the toilet, came by and picked up the second bucket and carried it to the kitchen. No need to return empty handed!

Dad caught the scene, and I was immediately whipped for allowing my mother to do my chores. Without benefit of trial, the sentence was executed. This incident would be considered cruel and unusual punishment by today's standard, but in that day it was not uncommon. Most fathers, particularly those of German descent, operated on a principle akin to the military which dictated that orders be carried out immediately and questions could be asked later. Even if my case could have been reviewed, and I had been found "not guilty," the lesson was impressed for future use. In adulthood, the boys of the family held no grudge realizing that our father, in every way, had a difficult task. As adults, they accepted the strict disciplinary code and jokingly referred, with appreciation, to the fact that they had been kept out of the prison system by it. It seems to me that the grown girls were not as generous with their appraisals in retrospect, for they too had been enrolled in the system and couldn't measure the responsibility as could the men. Anyway, it went with the territory!

There was no central heat in the house, and in wintertime a small pot belly stove was placed in the side of the kitchen opposite the range. It had its own chimney, bucket, and poker. I don't recall the make, but I do recall it was made in Pittsburgh. Between where the three legs fastened and the belly part of the stove was a two-inch wide circular shelf where one could put stocking feet that were cold or lay wet gloves or mittens to dry. An ash pit was above the ring. This stove also ate up, what seemed to a boy, an enormous amount of coal and spewed out buckets of ashes to be carried even beyond the coal house.

There was an additional heating stove in the living room area. It was a more slight model, with quite attractive iron work and nickel plated trim. It had a place to attach a heat pipe for heating an upper room. To my knowledge this was never done, but there was an overhead grate to a bedroom and heat naturally rose to it. Its habits were like the other two stoves, and it seemed to be a mixed blessing.

While thinking about this room, it occurred to me that two pictures hung there in large silver frames. One was a sizable photo of Dad when he was a clean-shaven young man. It was likely acquired when he was still single. The other was a colorful scene of a young couple who had, presumably, eloped and were being forgiven by her well-dressed Father, who stood by an attractive grey-saddled horse. There were probably other pictures, but none so well remembered.

The kitchen had a door to the back porch entrance which everybody used; it was never locked. It had one of the old square black locks which would have taken a three-inch long skeleton-type key, had anybody known its whereabouts. I recall the old porcelain knobs; one black on the outside, and one white inside. On the opposite side of the kitchen was another door with an etched glass pane, a pair of steps outside, and probably rusty hinges on the door, as no one used it.

On the same side was a cupboard, not built-in at that stage. It had two pieces with a shelf between the top and bottom doors where items, to be readily at hand, rested. A newspaper, school books, a pencil or two, a Bible, a recipe book, and other things rested there temporarily. On the end of the cupboard, out of reach of small fry, hung a black match box with an open bin on the bottom where matches would drop down from the inserted package. It contained strike-anywhere, "barn burner" matches. I think the matches were a nickel a box. The top half of the cupboard contained a motley assortment of porcelain or stoneware plates, cups, saucers, and serving dishes—no fine china. It would possibly have been imported from Europe or have been of early American manufacture. Dishes would not have consisted of sets, but likely would have had many sources, gathered possibly from auction sales. In any event, matching would not have been considered of importance, rather, they were utilitarian.

I seem to recall drawers in the bottom portion wherein would be kept a similar assortment of tableware, erroneously referred to as silverware. Beneath the drawers were two doors and shelves where mixing bowls and large serving dishes were kept. On the upper shelf of the top half could be found items from an earlier time, and a tin box where important papers were kept. I remember items remaining from a time when Dad had been township constable, including a pair of "brass knuckles," which were actually some other metal, probably aluminum. In any case, in the dictionary they are described as being for "rough fighting" and were a part of the defenses of a law officer. At some later date, they were classified as a concealed weapon and were outlawed. Another metal item recalled was a small plate with the inscription "Our Darling," apparently kept as a dubiously desirable memory from the casket of one of the infant children who had died. I never recalled any explanation for it.

Between the cupboard and the front door was the table, an expandable affair, probably extended to its limit with a fifth leg in the middle. There would have been a time when eight children sat at the table along with parents. Against the wall was a long bench on which the small fry sat. Chairs for the remainder would also have been assorted, including a couple without backs.

The larger girls helped with the serving. After supper, a tall kerosene lamp was placed in the center of the table, and the newspaper, school books, and papers would be in evidence.

Near the back door was a square washstand about thirty inches high. It had a drawer near the top which contained a soap supply, clean wash cloths, and possibly some sort of hand lotion of the day. A shelf near the floor had buckets to hold water for scrubbing floors and other uses. On the wall above, hung an old mirror which had belonged to our maternal grandmother. The glass was wavy and indicated very early fabrication. Beneath this hung an open metal comb case containing a couple of large combs and a brush. Girls may have had combs of their own on their dressers. As far as the boys were concerned, this was community property, as was the roller towel on a rack for hand washing.

To the left and rear of the wash stand was a dry sink, also from the same grandmother's home. It was made by her grandfather who was, among other things, a cabinet maker. It was approximately six feet long, made of pine wood, with two large doors hinged toward the ends. The top was deep set about four inches, and on the right side was a water bucket to be filled with well water from an outside pump. A long handled dipper floated on top—this was a family drinking vessel. The remainder of the top was kept available for whatever food preparation was in progress, from slicing bread to preparing vegetables, or storing canned goods in the cooling process.

Below were two shelves for storing such things as a metal round container with a lid for sugar, which usually came in five or ten pound bags; one or more of these bags would also be stored here. Bread, which was cooled on the warming tank, would also be stored here. Here was also the rolling pin, wrapped in the sides of the latest twenty-five pound flour bag. It was unrolled on the table where dough for pie crusts or cookies was prepared.

Behind the range was the flue cupboard. The bottom shelf would have been further from the floor than the distance between the higher shelves. All the shelves were set back from the door to allow for a broom and mop to stand or hang. On the floor was a couple of nested scrub buckets with brushes and cloths or rags. Also, the supply of kerosene, or coal oil as some referred to it, was kept in a one-gallon container with spout for pouring a thin stream into lamps. On the higher shelves were a tin can with detachable lid in which was kept tallow for greasing leather shoes, any shoe polishing brushes, and equipment for "fine" shoes. Perhaps a small supply of corn to pop, or dry beans, a handy screw driver, a pair of pliers, and a tack hammer for small repair jobs, would also be there. A small basket of cloths for easy access, and other small convenience items might also be found.

These descriptives would have covered the bulk of what was contained in the kitchen. There was no overhead light, nor were there any wall cupboards which became essential objects in later kitchens.

Especially in winter, the kitchen was what we would call the family room. Sometimes, the school children would retire to the living room for homework.

Two doors led off the kitchen on its south side into two small rooms, which completed the size of the original three room one-story house. One of these was the parent's bedroom. Behind the door, which was made of vertical hand-planed boards, was a strip of wood fastened horizontally to the hidden studs and having double hooks for hanging clothes. Here hung the couple of "Sunday" dresses and one man's suit. Set on the floor in the corner was a shotgun and a small bore rifle. Under-clothing would be in the dresser, which had a mounted mirror, and on the top would be the large family Bible and whatever toilet articles my parents possessed. I seem to recall a religious picture on the wall, but can't further describe it.

The other door led into a room of the same size containing a large cherry chest of drawers and a library table. On at least one and possibly two walls, were horizontal strips and double hooks or nails for hanging clothes. Though I don't remember it, I was told that my maternal grandmother slept there with one or two grandchildren. She died before I was born.

After the turn of the century, Dad built a two-story addition on the house which could be accessed through a door cut in the end of grandmother's room and set at right angles. Under the stairs to the bedrooms was a much needed storage space. The only furniture in it was a large pine chest, also made by grandmother's father. This storage space later became the bathroom.

More horizontal strips for hanging clothes were on the east wall. There was also a "rag bag" with odds and ends of materials for patching clothes. Some of the material would have come from left over material used in making "haps." The origin of the word "hap" is not known to me, nor could I find information about it

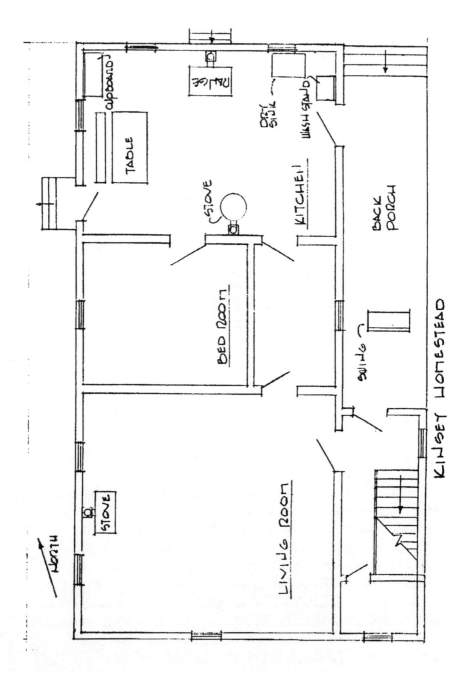

First floor plan of Homestead.

in brief research. It could have been called that because of the haphazard appearance of patches, utilizing whatever material was available, which could be pieced together in odd design to make the top side of a bed cover. Beneath this could be cotton batting, or perhaps old blankets, which had been worn thin through use and washings. The bottom lining would be something of a printed cotton bolt goods with any amount of variations, mostly determined by availability. Then, at regular spacing, five or six inches apart, the entire collection would be knotted from top to lining with wool yarn and tied on the top side.

The addition to the house likely required months of part-time work. The second story consisted of a small room on the rear side with one window. Above the sloping stairway ceiling was another small storage area, with a trap door access to an attic. It was seldom used since the other larger bedroom had an access door to the attic over the three room section, which was much more easily reached. A small hallway with one window led from the top of the stairway to the larger bedroom. It had three windows and ample room for two double beds, a dresser, and an old-fashioned wash stand with two drawers above two doors, and a towel bar to the rear. Here again, were horizontal wood strips for hanging clothes.

All of the window and door trim was cherry, since at that time cherry was not considered a premium wood. Much of that trim still exists today; though it is covered with many coats of paint. Throughout the house were baseboards about six inches high, held at the bottom by quarter-round. The interior of the add-on was lathed with thin wood lath, about one and one half inches wide and long enough to reach from stud to stud with narrow cracks between the lath. The undercoating of plaster consisted of lime, sand, and hog hair, which helped to hold it together. It would have been applied with a plasterer's trowel about ten inches long and four inches wide with an open-end handle on the user's side. The plaster would have been of such a consistency as to be forced through the cracks between the lath, overhanging and making a tight bond when dried. After the drying, a finish coat of smooth white lime would be plastered over, making the room much brighter. This would be exposed sometimes for many years until it became marred, and then it would be painted or wallpapered. Dad's brother, Alfred W. Kinsey, was a plasterer; and I have little doubt that he did the plastering.

The exterior would have been vertical or slanting sheathing boards, and horizontal lap siding. No insulation was used in those days, apparently because heating costs were nominal. The add-on roof was probably tar paper which was later covered with tin roofing.

Free Water

We drank it from a shallow well,
Drawn through a pump of wood.
An easy distance from the house
This faithful helper stood.

The thirsts of man and animal
Were slaked for many a year,
And water used for washing
Was carried forth from here.

No monthly bill was coming.
No filter bed was found.
The liquid simply issued
From streams down under ground.

From bottom up the chasm,
Round levels laid in stone,
The top, a large ceramic tile
Extending two feet down.

Along about the summer late,
The water level fell.
The family head decided,
T'was time to clean the well.

Because the space had limits,
The worker need be small.
With scoop and bucket dangling,
He was lowered past the wall.

To gather muck and pebbles
That seeped in with the flow.
The surface seemed so far away
When looked at from below.

The cleaning finally ended
In long and dreadful time.
T'was then to purify the floor
By sprinkling it with lime.

The lad now fixed the rope around
His anxious, beating chest
Was safely drawn—ascending
To a world of daylight blest.

The well, no longer useful,
Was filled—now out of sight.
The lad, now old, when anxious,
Looks up to see the Light.

W.K. 12/92

CHAPTER 5

The Cellar

The cellar was underneath the kitchen and was accessible only by going out the back door, down four steps to ground level, and one quarter way around the kitchen, where stood a sloping pair of outside doors. At the bottom of four more steps was an inside door. The floor was earthen, beaten by years of tramping to a smooth surface.

At different places along the walls were placed wooden timbers which probably had once been railroad ties, since there was an abandoned lumbering road bed nearby. On top of these would be wooden planks to keep the various necessities off the ground. I don't recall there being any water on the floor in my early days. Much later, it seemed the stone drain, over nearly level ground, must have filled with sediment and a sump pump was installed.

One of the things thus elevated was an old dry sink which was used to store canned goods in glass jars. Here would be found green beans, beets, corn, berries (both blue and black), pickles, peaches, tomatoes, etc. Though the cupboard had two shelves and the sunken top, it could not hold all of the canned goods to last the winter for a large family of hungry kids. There was also a hanging shelf, consisting of one large wide board suspended by heavy wire from the joist. In a corner was a small barrel (probably thirty gallon size) containing sauerkraut. This would have been made in the fall by slicing cabbage on a wooden frame with metal knife blades, over which ran a four-sided wooden, open ended box about three inches high. It ran on a track, and into it the head of cabbage was placed. As the head grew smaller, a knobbed board fit into the box so as to avoid cutting the hand. After an inch or so of sliced cabbage built up in the barrel, it was then tamped with a wooden stomper until the mass was covered with liquid, then another layer was cut and added. A portion of salt was sprinkled on each layer. When the barrel was filled to the desired level, usually somewhere near the top, it was covered with two semicircular oak boards which made a circle slightly smaller than the circumference of the barrel. These were weighted down by a clean, rounded creek stone weighing probably ten pounds. When the mixture had properly aged, the board and stone would have been removed and kept. "Kraut" was available into the spring. Gallon milk crocks rested on the floor, fresh milk in one crock, cream in another. All were covered with old plates or boards. This was the only refrigeration. Countless trips had to be made from the kitchen.

Next to the liquid barrel was a "dry" barrel which would have been used for shipping or storing anything not covered by liquid. Examples of such contents could be dishes, small hardware objects, fruit, etc. The staves in this type were not tightly fitted, and hence were not air tight. Two, three, or more of the type would be filled with winter apples which came from a tree standing on the line between the house lot and an additional one acre parcel, which Dad bought separately for a handy truck patch of various usages. The apples, being a winter variety, were very hard when picked by hand, since fallen apples were bruised and would spoil before they would ripen. In storage, they would last far into the winter and were a source of very scarce fresh fruit. Apple butter crocks would be in storage also.

It seems fitting here to digress and add some history of the apple tree. As it now seems, it probably measured sixteen inches or so from bark-to-bark. With a little help from some prop, or a boost from a companion, a boy or girl could reach the lower branches and scale the remainder. Need it be said that the old tree was a mecca for kids? Jungle gyms were unheard of in this time and place. The apple tree, however, was its precursor for this family. In the fall, half shocks of corn stalks, tied separately after husking and kept for cow feed, were stood around the tree and bound at the center circumference against fierce winter storms.

Though it never happened to me, the two older brothers who were born in tandem (Ford and Glenn), as were my next older brother (Frank) and me, related the story. These kinds of boys made a team. They were about two years apart, age wise; and as the story went, what one could not conjure up, the other could. When the older team had committed some unsanctioned activity calling for justice, mercy was not usually a part of the occurrence. To aid in meting out such justice, Dad would take out his pocket knife, hand it to one of the culprits, and demand a suitable switch from the old apple tree. On at least one occasion they were sent back because the proffered object did not meet the required standard of the recipient. It was too limber, even though used in conjunction with the ever present razor strop. Dad believed in the Biblical wisdom of Solomon who said, "He that spareth his rod hateth his son; but he that loveth him chasteneth him betimes (Proverbs 13:24)." Years later, when the old tree died and had to be cut down, the brothers intoned that it should have been done years before. There was no remorse. Back to the cellar.

On the back cellar wall area was a large potato bin which held as many as fifty bushels of potatoes. One winter rats apparently came up the drain and tunneled through the potatoes. There was no evidence of it in sight, but in time a terrible odor of rotting permeated the air. On investigation, it was found that the tunneling had left much rotten chewing underneath. The entire crop had to be removed and damaged parts destroyed. It was an awful and malodorous mess. The rats were eradicated, mostly by trapping. I don't recall ever seeing evidence of rats there again.

In the fall as many fresh vegetables as could be accommodated were brought from the garden and used as long as they would keep in good condition. These were mostly root crops.

A small keg of apple vinegar would have been in evidence there. Freshly pressed apples were the source, into which, from the previous keg, "mother" would have been added. This is a sort of gelatinous substance resembling a combination of tapioca pudding and frog eggs. It was used to cause fermentation of vinegar or wine. It was stringy, slimy, and contained useful bacteria.

Sometimes in the fall and early winter, a barrel of hard cider could be seen. I recall one incident relating to the hard cider. As stated elsewhere, our house was never locked for it was seldom void of people. The outhouse, stable, and cellar were, however, locked; and keys for those locks hung in the kitchen. One Sunday evening, after the chores were done, I had locked the buildings and put the keys in my pocket while going to Christian Endeavor with Mom. Meanwhile, Dad came back from visiting and brought along two or three gentlemen friends—of whom he had many when cider was on tap. Alas! The cellar was locked; the one key being at church. Let me haste to say that Dad was by no means an alcoholic, as he could afford neither sufficient liquor, nor the time away from work to imbibe. He would, however, take a drink in moderation. Doubtless, as thirst mounted, patience grew thin. When we finally came home from church, he was very upset and probably embarrassed before his friends and would have whipped me for being so careless. It was one of the few times I knew Mom to talk back to him; she dared him to lay a hand on me. He didn't! I never want to be guilty of putting him down for he had many virtues of which you may read elsewhere.

Renovated house - taken in 1993—At right, edge of sloping cellar door—access to the only refrigeration.

CHAPTER 6

Garden

Gardening was a practice which seems to have been enjoyed by our parents and endured by the children. It may have given the parents a relaxing change from the daily demands and given way to contemplation. It was also a necessity in providing much needed food. In our scheme of things, the garden was generally divided into three segments: the first of which consisted of three beds; the second, a larger truck patch; and the third, a still larger area somewhat generally removed from the house.

The area of the beds began just beyond the well and was closest to the house. A bed had, on three sides, a trench or walk so that one could reach the farther area without treading the loose soil. The bottoms of the walk would be about a foot deeper than the growing surface. The sides of it would be tapered away from the bottom, and the soil would be patted into place. Leaf lettuce was generally grown on this slope, making it easily accessible for picking and tending, and to hold the soil in place. Beds would be readied by spading under manure. Larger areas would be plowed. On these beds the smaller, and perhaps more tender, plants would be grown. Here would be rows of radishes, beets, and carrots far enough apart to hoe between. Onions were planted in rows closer together and would be started with "sets," bought, and ranging in size from that of a large pea to that of hickory nut. A special hoe was usually made—a cut down size from a worn hoe, leaving the center rib little more than an inch in width. As soon as the stem of the onion was firm enough to be dipped in a salt cellar, they would be pulled and eaten, with the tops cut off. Left to grow, they had bulbs on the root end and would usually be left in the ground until fall. The onions would then be dried and stored for winter. Parsnips could be grown in such a bed. They were not a favorite food for the children, although they were more palatable if fried than if stewed. They could be left in the ground to be dug up as needed. Peas could be planted in rows as could low-growing beans, which could either be snapped green, or at maturity dried and shelled. Pole beans would vine and were usually planted in the truck patch, and pyramiding piles would be joined between rows.

In a second bed, tomatoes would be set in; sometimes they would be staked and tied, and other times left to grow on the ground with straw to keep the fruit off the soil. Vines needed to be trimmed of "suckers," lest there be too many branches for the root supply.

The third bed would be mostly planted with cabbage; heads could be cut off during summer, and brussels sprouts would grow on the root top. When fall arrived, the root would be pulled with the head attached. Three rows of these would be tightly packed. Two rows would be set on a second tier, and one row on the third. About eighteen inches from the bottom row, a trench would be dug, the soil from which would be heaped upon the rows which had, by now, been covered with straw, the entire heap tapering to the top and forming a sort of elongated pyramid. The heap would likely be twelve or fourteen feet long and six feet wide. Some heads with roots attached would have been taken to the cellar and used until consumed, or they began to spoil. At that time the pyramid would be opened up and a new supply taken out. By then, the entire mass would be frozen to frost depth, and the opening would need to be closed in again.

At the edge of the bed, nearest the property line, would be perennial plants such as rhubarb, horse radish, and tansy. This plant, according to Webster, is used in medicines. That may well be so, but it was Mom's only defense against an infestation of ants. It was simply cut off and placed along the trail discouraging the onslaught.

The truck patch had its most important function in growing

sweet corn for corn-on-the-cob in July and August. During this time it could also be cut off and canned or dried. Dried, it was easy to keep, even in colonial times. To my memory, it was best used in combination dishes or soup, but could be served stewed. Like dried beans, it needed to be soaked overnight. Should any of it be left in the fall, it could be fed to pigs, or ground into whatever dry feed was provided for stock. Popcorn was also grown. Along the lot line, a couple of currant bushes grew providing red berries for making jelly.

Mom — circa 20's

Cucumbers were allowed more room to vine here and could be harvested at the proper size for pickles, which could be canned or put down in brine in crocks. They could also be sliced, when fresh, with onions for salad. Perhaps a row of early variety potatoes would be planted in order to have them close by. If they were not eaten with the jackets on, they would be scraped rather than pared, as the skin was thin and tender. A couple of rows of pole beans were always in order, and their place in the scheme of things is mentioned elsewhere. Any sort of beans in the early stages could be used in a mixture of cream potatoes. Current dietary experts keep reiterating that we should, even today, be getting more protein from beans rather than red meats. Turnip seed would have been broadcast at the time of last cultivating corn.

If Mom could arrange it, the row closest to the house would be planted with flowers, variegated to her choice. Early on, Dad preferred to have it planted with something edible. He may have felt like a comrade of mine in W.W. II, who insisted that an Italian farmer wanted nothing to do with an animal unless he could work it, milk it, breed it, and eat it; afterward selling the hide. Later in life, when the pressures of family support diminished, Dad relented. He mellowed in various ways as he aged. While I was fearful of him in my early life, we became fast friends as I matured.

The largest of the patches generally would be farthest from the house on a separate parcel of land. It would include the potato patch which is described under the Food Chapter. It would contain the corn field, meaning of course, field corn. The preparation of this area was done by different local farmers who had teams. They would plow and harrow, as well as "drill" in the corn seed and fertilize with a corn planter. As the corn appeared in the rows, it was soon necessary to cultivate it with a single horse and a five bladed cultivator, going on each side of the corn, once in each direction. As there were stones in the soil, the cultivator would sometimes cover or bend over a stalk. The stalks had to be uncovered or straightened by a boy following with a hoe. When I was still quite small, I was relegated to this job. On the one occasion recalled, the man engaged was seventy-plus years old and was driving a bay mare that had previously been retired from a larger farm. He had only a single rein which was forked at the front and had half of it attached to each side of the horse's bit. This meant he could only jerk the line with no sense of direction, and talk to the horse, which he did incessantly. "Gee Bess, gee Bess" or "haw Bess, Bess, Bess, Bess." Bess became immune to the babble and went where her years of experience had taught her. The driver, Mr. Bush, was a kindly old man whose ever present tennis shoes were right before my eyes as I followed him, uncovering the tender corn stalks. Incidentally, no older person was ever called by his or her first name, but rather by "Mr." or "Mrs.", and spoken to as "Sir" or "Ma'am." Both man and horse were inflicted with an over abundance of gas. Sometimes separately, and sometimes in unison it would be wafted into the air. Only with a change of direction or a shift of breeze would it dissipate.

Periodically, cultivating was required to keep down weeds and aerate the soil. Between cultivation, it was deemed necessary to hoe the corn by hand between the stalks. Although later on this operation was eliminated, it was in vogue at the time.

When fall arrived, the stalks were cut with a long knife which would reach below the knees. The stalk was held by one hand while the other hand would wield the knife. A "saddle" would be made by taking four rooted stalks from two opposite rows and twisting their tops together between the rows. Severed stalks would be set up against the saddle until a shock was cut. This would be tied with binder twine and let to stand until the stalks and leaves dried. The stock would then be pulled over, after the saddle support was cut. Usually two men would kneel, one on either side of the shock and husk the ears, using a hand held tool to separate the husk at its top and peel it off the ear. The stalk was held in one hand, and with the other the ear was snapped off and thrown into a pile. When all ears had been husked, the stalks were already divided into two piles and tied separately. These were ready to be hauled to the barn, or, in our case a stable, where they were chopped a few at a time in winter by a corn cutter, and thrown in a manger where the cow would eat the leaves.

As the corn grew, pumpkin seeds were planted by the stalks so that by the time cultivating stopped, vines could spread out at will. Pies were a favorite in fall. I don't recall Mom ever canning pumpkin. Excess ones were cut up into small pieces and fed to the cow with the dry feed at milking time. Some, of course, were made into jack-o-lanterns and later fed to the stock.

CHAPTER 7

Food

The acquiring, storing, preparation, and consumption of food was a most vital operation, differing in the extreme from current practice. A great majority of it was formed on the premises. Perhaps by volume, more potatoes were consumed than any other thing. Few meals did not include them. Let's try to consider from whence and how they came. Probably two hundred yards from the house on a slightly higher elevation Dad owned a parcel, acquired in two transactions, being about fifteen acres in all. Probably three acres of it were covered by second growth woods, the remainder in fields. A nearby farmer with a team of horses would be hired to plow up the desired plots. The potato patch would be of varying size up to an acre. The corn field was larger, varying in size up to seven acres or so. An area that had been plowed for several years may be planted in oats or wheat, with grass or clover sown with it so that after the wheat was harvested there would be a ground cover to become next year's hay field. Crops were rotated.

Planting potatoes was particularly difficult if sod had been plowed under. During harrowing or scoring out a row with a single blade plow, pieces of sod would turn up and would need to be placed back in the row, under the potato seed and upside down.

About the seed: Rarely were seed potatoes bought, and then only to have a new and better strain. Most were the white variety. At planting time whole potatoes were cut so that each piece had an eye where the sprout would appear. The remaining part of the piece sustained the sprout until it took root and appeared above ground.

Dad preferred to have the seed laid with the eye upward on

the bottom of the scored furrow. Seed was placed about ten inches apart, the distance being gauged by the foot of the planter. A hoe was used to cover the seed lightly with soil. Atop this, phosphate dust would be sprinkled out of a bucket by hand. This again was covered, bringing the row up to the surface.

The potatoes remaining from winter would sprout in spring and had to be "sprouted" lest the sprout consume the potato. Old potatoes would be used until the supply was exhausted or until new ones could be dug, usually in July or August, depending on planting time and nature.

When the potatoes came up, alas, weeds and grass came up with them, necessitating another operation. The cultivator had small blades or shovels arranged in a triangular fashion with one in the center; farther back, two on line; and still farther back, four on line. This covered the area and had to be pulled by a horse on each side of the row, as close to the plant as was safe without damaging it. Between the potatoes there would still be grass or weeds which needed to be taken out with a hoe. This whole operation took place periodically, depending on the growth of weeds and the hardness of the soil baked by the sun.

When the seed grew sizable plants, potato bugs began to appear. The cure for this problem was for a boy to go along the rows with a short stick in one hand and a small can of kerosene in the other. The bug was simply knocked into the can. There were varieties of bugs. One was a pinkish soft-shelled one, another a yellow hard-shelled one. No matter the type, they had to be eliminated. Later on Dad bought a duster which was a square box-like thing carried with a shoulder strap and cranked on the right side. Dust was blown through a flexible tube with a nozzle turned upward to spray the under side of the leaves.

About midsummer a two-shovel plow was pulled to "hill" the row and allow the potatoes to grow nearer the surface.

If Dad was between jobs and a horse could be rented, he would do the cultivating—a one horse operation. If he was working, especially at his trade of stone masonry, both horse and driver would be rented.

When the plants died, toward fall, a one-shovel plow would be used to plow out the potatoes and expose them to sight. They were simply gathered up in buckets and bagged to be hauled to the bin. Sometimes, after a rain, others would show up and a second picking would take place. Every size of potato was picked. Really small ones could be separated and cooked with the "jackets" on, but more likely they were cooked in an iron kettle over an outside fire, mashed, and added to feed for pigs, chickens, or dogs. Dogs were not particularly fond of them, but, like the kids, they ate what they were served.

Let us turn now to the way in which potatoes were served. The small ones mentioned above were sometimes boiled with the jackets on and served with the meal. Salt, pepper, homemade butter, or gravy was added. The diner had the choice of taking off the skins or "eating skins and all" as an old song said. They might be peeled, boiled, and mashed. In that event, if any were left over, they appeared the following day as fried cakes. Sometimes they were creamed with green beans. If they were baked in the coal range oven (having been thoroughly scrubbed of course) one had the choice again of eating the delicious skins. Most chose to do that. One of our favorites was thinly sliced raw potatoes, fried to golden brown in a large iron skillet where they were turned often, and always fried in lard. Another favorite was to have them pared, boiled, cooled, and diced. Eggs would be broken over them and possibly some left-over ham diced into the mix, which was then fried. In summer, of course, mustard, and sometimes diced celery was served. Sometimes on a winter evening they would be pared, thinly sliced, and laid on the hot range lids. Slight salting and turning produced a delicious treat. We had never heard of potato chips like the ones sold today.

In summer a variety of fresh vegetables was on hand. In winter, canned vegetables, fruits, berries, and cherries were in store. Pork was always available in some form. Chickens could be killed at will, usually for Sunday dinner. On Saturday Mom would decide to have chicken and would put water on to boil. The boys all took their turn, at some stage, to decide the fate of the particular chicken, run it down, and take it with the ax to the chopping block in the alley, and lop off its head. It would then flop around furiously by reflex action and "bleed out." Roosters were always kept to a count of one to avoid constant war. If there were no extra males, a hen would be chosen for dinner. When she had kicked her last, boiling water would be put in a bucket where the chicken was dipped until the feathers pulled easily. When plucking was done, Mom would take a ball of crumpled newspapers, lift the lid on the range, and drop in the paper. By its flame, the hair would be singed off. If the boy were large and knowledgeable enough, he would then draw the entrails. Mom always wanted to scrub and cut up the carcass in her own way; unless, of course, it would be stuffed and roasted. Earlier on it was certain one chicken would not suffice. I was on the end of the line, and the size of the family had dwindled.

In spring the first fresh vegetable was dandelion greens, dug from a field of low grass. At this season it was considered sport to hunt for morels, which we also called mushrooms. They would be found in wooded areas. They were usually fried in butter and were delicious.

In summer Dad and the larger kids, if they were available, would go for berries, taking along the dogs and the mattock. If a groundhog were treed, it could be shot with a pistol which Dad carried. If it holed, it would be dug out and shot in the hole. It would be drawn, the cavity filled with fern, and a double-pointed stick shoved through its hind feet making a carrying handle. Immediately when home was reached, the hide was removed and the carcass soaked in salt water on the cellar floor. Next day Mom would cut it in pieces, par-boil it, roll it in crumbs or cornmeal, then fry it. Many people would frown upon eating it, but woodchucks are strict vegetarians and, properly cooked, make a delicious main course.

When the family was at its largest Mom baked twice weekly, all the large oven would hold. When kids came home from school on baking day, they were allowed a slice of fresh bread and applebutter to stave off starvation until suppertime. While in the baking business, she usually baked pies—apple, berry, cherry, and pumpkin. Occasionally, she baked cake and, rarely, cookies, probably for lack of time.

Flour was always bought in a twenty-five pound bag, and each baker had her own favorite brand. The head of one family in town managed a company store in an adjoining coal town. He managed to have a supply of the empty bags for his wife's favorite brand. When a bag of any brand was broken, he simply poured the remainder in an empty bag of his wife's brand and delivered it home when flour was on the want list. There was no evidence that she knew the difference.

Before leaving for whatever sort of manual labor he was engaged in at the time, Dad ate an early breakfast. It always consisted of hearty fare such as pork chops or ham and eggs, always potatoes in some form, maybe a small serving of oatmeal. Buckwheat or corn cakes or flapjacks were often served, usually with "Karo" corn syrup and sausage. Puffed or flaky cereal did not fill the bill. He did not care for toast, but homemade bread and butter with what he called a "second spread" of jam, jelly, or apple butter rounded out the meal, except for his one daily serving of coffee. He usually carried an aluminum two-drawer bucket, the bottom half of which held water, hedging against the lack of any where he may be working. Mom packed it while he ate.

Sandwiches were the main stay with perhaps a pickle, an apple, or a generous cut of pie, usually berry or fruit.

There was rarely a gathering of the clan for breakfast. The older boys or girls may be day-working somewhere in the summertime.

It should be noted that most of what was eaten was available as the result of our combined efforts and the generosity of God and nature. On hand were milk, eggs, pork, chickens, game, and bounteous garden produce. There were, however, some necessities which could not be provided. For these someone went to Mrs. Rehm's store which was conveniently and diagonally across the road. Here are items shown in her day ledger under my father's account, which showed debit and credit columns. The first page reviewed was for the period July 12, 1920, to August 14, 1920. Some things are omitted because of illegible writing or some brand name not now recognized.

July 12: Crackers 20¢, rice 15¢, vinegar 20¢, soap 10¢, sugar 96¢, cake 20¢, Castor Oil 35¢, cheese 25¢.

July 13: Milk (evaporated) 10¢, oil (kerosene) 25¢, cakes 20¢, sugar 72¢.

July 14: Cake 12¢, applebutter 55¢, oats 15¢.

July 15: Coffee 55¢, crackers 24¢

July 16: Bread 18¢, cakes 15¢, bread 18¢, soap 19¢, bread 36¢.

July 17: Syrup 18¢, tacks 6¢, mild 10¢

July 19: Baked beans 40¢, rice 30¢, mild 10¢, applebutter 55¢, crackers 24¢, tomatoes 15¢, milk 10¢, bread 36¢, matches 10¢, bread 36¢.

July 20: Corn 40¢, bread 18¢.

July 21: Crisp (?) 15¢, milk 20¢, Crisp 15¢.

July 22: Butter 45¢, flour $2.15

July 23: Macaroni 20¢, salt 8¢, oil 25¢, oats 50¢

July 24: Coffee 55¢, Crisp 19¢.

July 26: Vinegar 20¢, bread 18¢, cake 20¢, bread 18¢.

July 29: Cakes 15¢, broom $1.10, baked beans 40¢.

July 30: Applebutter 55¢, oats 18¢.

Aug 02: Bread 36¢, eggs 25¢, yeast 10¢, vinegar 25¢.

Aug 03: Bread 18¢, soap 80¢, Puffed wheat 17¢, sugar 60¢

Aug 04: Rice 18¢, vinegar 20¢, raisins 35¢, yeast 10¢.

Aug 06: Lace 25¢, cakes 10¢, baked beans 18¢, flour $2.15.

Aug 07: Gums (jars?) 10¢, salt 20¢, pants 75¢, coffee 55¢, sugar 50¢.

Aug 09: Sugar $1.50, gums 10¢.

Aug 10: Lace 10¢, Crisp 15¢, potatoes 25¢, bread 36¢, soap 9¢.

Aug 11: Sugar 60¢, soap 10¢, matches 10¢, sugar 60¢, oil 25¢, stock food 30¢, Crisp, cake 20¢, baked beans 18¢, starch 15¢.

Aug 12: Soda 15¢, gum 10¢.

Aug 13: Crisp 15¢, flour $2.15, bread 18¢, baked beans 20¢.

Aug 14: Shredded wheat 20¢, thread 12¢, baked beans 36¢, sugar $1.50.

In review, we may speculate about some entries. It was a surprise to find cakes numerous times. They may have been bought for Dad's bucket. Vinegar, as stated elsewhere, was usually in a keg in the cellar. Applebutter was usually homemade. Crisp is a mystery. Oats (rolled) came in different sized boxes, hence the variation in price. Butter must have been bought because the cow was "dry" or it simply did not last to the next possible churning. The store bread must have filled in between bakings. Oil (kerosene), found in the ledger repeatedly, was for lamps and rarely for starting a hurry-up fire. It was bought only a gallon at a time and carried in a can with a small potato stuck on the spout to keep it from leaking enroute.

Perhaps with regard to any change in grocery purchases, it would be well to say that Mom's last pregnancy had ended on April 10th of 1920, with the arrival of a stillborn daughter named Lisa. She may have been obliged to diminish her work schedule for the summer. Additionally, since the early children aspired only to a grade school education, as was generally done at that time, they left home at an early age. The place where they worked may also have provided room and board.

In the store ledger for May, 1921, a few new entries were found. Oleo was priced at thirty to forty cents. It came uncolored and looked like lard. With it came a small capsule of coloring which had to be mixed or kneaded in. This, we understand, was because of a strange quirk in the law probably resulting from a dairy lobby of that day. Wax was also a new entry, and since its price was only three cents, it is presumed to have been sealing wax. Tomatoes were canned in tin cans, and hot wax sealed the lids. Seeds also appeared (either garden or flower). "Pickles" cost twenty-one cents, probably for quart jar. Corn flakes were a rare purchase. Catsup also appeared at fifteen cents. What appeared to read as "buns" were priced at thirty-five cents, probably per dozen. Sardines, thirty cents; butter, forty-five cents; broom, $1.10: and combs, twenty cents.

The store bill was always of great concern for Dad. Sometimes by spring it would seem, to him, to be a sizable amount. As he would begin to work at his trade at a higher wage, the bill would be diminished by midsummer. Then he would save money toward the following winter's bill. This was the only thing I ever knew of him to buy on credit. He also was very concerned to have sufficient funds to pay the property tax. As was true with most people in that day, if money were not on hand, nothing was bought and charged to the future. There was no government welfare in those days, nor would he have been on it had it existed. When, later, it came into being, he never applied for, or received from, the "dole."

Though I could not find any trace of it in my short perusal of Mrs. Rehm's ledger, something reminded me of the control of houseflies. First, of course, was the swatter which was made of the metal screening used in making a window screen. For the swatter, it was cut in about a three by five inch piece, edged with a sewn on cloth, and attached to a foot long wire looped handle. Screens were not generally attached to the window frame but were on two separate wood frames combined in a sliding, expandable unit. When fresh air was needed, a window sash was raised, the unit set under it and expanded to close the opening, and the window lowered on it. There were also sticky traps. A piece of thin cardboard or heavy paper about 12 x 8 inches was covered with a semi-liquid adherent, and had a removable paper covering. This was laid on a flat surface where the fly could land and await its demise. There was also a hanging variety which came in a two inch long tube. The sticky paper was coiled inside with a loop string attached to one end for hanging, while the other end was attached to the bottom of the tube. The strip would uncoil easier when heated. The loop end was attached to the ceiling with a thumb tack which was held in place while the coil was extended to about eighteen inches. The empty tube, still attached, would be weighted to stretch the coil, and presto!, a double-barreled death trap!

There was also an entry in the ledger for "Black Flag." Though the supposition has not been confirmed, the name may have been derived from the name of the pirate flag, which was black cloth with a white skull and crossbones. There was also a yellow and black combination flag, indicating the presence of cholera on board the ship flying such a flag. A product by the name was recently available in liquid aerosol. Memory indicates that earlier in the century there was a product composed of a black absorbable paper, which was used in water to form a poison liquid for killing flies.

CHAPTER 8

Clothing

It would be shocking to most people today to realize how little clothing our family had. For the most part, school children had two outfits. One would be worn while the other one was being washed, ironed, and mended. I remember an instance when we received a dry barrel of used clothing from a distant family whom I never knew. If there were no size or sex to fit, the clothing would be given to another family. Nothing went to waste. The usual outfit for boys was knee length pants, knicker style, with suspenders. Possibly, three shirts were available. In winter one-piece union suits, which reached to the ankles, were worn and were covered with black stockings which extended above the knees, and held by elastic garters. Shoes always covered the ankles and were regularly greased with beef tallow or sheep tallow, if available. This was kept in a tin can which would be heated on the back of the coal range until warm enough to liquify. It would be applied with a cloth, and the shoe would be held over the open flame until no more would be absorbed into the leather. These were snow wear too, as arctics were not generally available.

The girls generally had two or three gingham dresses, possibly a skirt or jumper with shoulder straps, and a blouse. Under garments were either cotton or light wool and generally hand-made. I do not specifically recall the footwear, but it was probably a cuban heel type, which would be laced and probably four to eight inches high.

For fabricating and repairing, Mom had a "Wheeler" treadle sewing machine, which would drop into the cabinet and be covered with the hinged work table top. The treadle was levered to a wheel which had a round leather drive belt attached to the head of the machine when it was raised for sewing. It had two drawers on either side of the knee hole over the treadle. In these drawers were thread, buttons, scissors, and one or two attachments for special jobs on the machine. Mom did not classify herself as a seamstress, but could make over a simple pattern and repair, repair, repair. Patched knees and elbows were usually the uniform of the day. We were taught not to be ashamed of patches as most children had some. Clothing must, however, be kept clean.

There were some stock food mills who bagged food in gingham patterns, and many of the girls and women of the time wore dresses made of these bags. Sometimes they could go to the mill and find different patterns from which to select. Many older ladies of today have related the experience of wearing dresses made from this source.

Of course, all clothing had to be washed. Most children would have two or three outfits which could be changed midweek. Often these outfits were the Sunday wear, too. Washing at our house was done on Monday and was no quick and easy task. In winter, before going to school, we boys would bring the folding washstand into the kitchen from the back porch. It had a drop down shelf on either side of the standing hand wringer. On one stand was a galvanized tub, and on the other a tub with wooden staves. A copper boiler with lid, about two feet long and fifteen inches high, would be set on the range top and would be filled with water to heat. The warming tank on the range would be filled the previous night. The tea kettle was always on the range, and perhaps another kettle with a lid would be set for warming the wash water, which cooled in the washing process. All white clothes usually needed to be boiled to be clean. After boiling, these would be lifted out with a long stick and carried in a large pan to the wooden tub, which by now had warm water and a washboard, on which a bar of soap was in a slot at the top. Sometimes this was homemade from grease drippings and lye. If finances permitted, the soap was Fels-naptha, purchased at the general store.

In the tub, the white clothes from the boiler would then be hand rubbed on the board and wrung into the galvanized tub, which had rinse water in it. Clothes would be wrung and the water returned to the tub from which they came via a flipper drain. After rinsing and wringing, the clothes would be thrown in a large basket to be carried later to the outside clothes line and hung to dry, or freeze, as the temperature determined. Then dark clothes would be rubbed from the wooden tub after some hot water was added from the boiler. The process would be repeated. All this time the range would need coal, a time or two. Two or more outfits from each of the family of eight or ten made for a day's work. Also, meals still had to be prepared, simple easy ones, if possible.

In freezing weather, clothes on the outside lines simply froze after little drying. They were brought in stiff and hung on a ten fingered rack which was fastened to the frame board on the chimney cupboard. The rack dropped down against the frame when not in use.

Following this, when school children came home, it was their duty to carry the used water outside in buckets until the weight was diminished and the remainder could be carried out in the tubs, which, after rinsing, would be hung on the back porch. The wringer stand would also be stored there. Any spillage was mopped up, and that phase would be completed.

Roberta Schwarz, who was mentioned in the Mom Chapter, reminded me of something I must have forgotten—to the effect that Mom had taken in washings for awhile. My brother Ford had four cottages which he rented to summer vacationers from Pittsburgh. Roberta recalled that Mom washed and ironed for them, as well as for a Mrs. Ankney, who lived close by and was in poor health. I have no way now of correlating the times, but it must have happened after the arrival of electric service, and after the family size had dwindled. Ford had given her a used "Horton" washer which had an agitator shaped like the lights over a pawn shop. It had three inverted metal cups on the ends of three arms. These rotated gently and rose and fell on the clothes, exerting vacuum on the return. It had a motor driven wringer. Even so, a less energetic woman might have declined accepting yet another duty.

Next, of course, items to be worn needed ironed. The irons were heated on the range. Handles were detachable lest they get too hot to touch. To test the iron for temperature, a finger would be wet with saliva and touched to the iron. If it sizzled, it was hot enough. Before setting it on the cloth, it would be run over a waxed cloth to clean it and give it a gliding characteristic. Girls could begin this process while supper was in progress, or divide other details such as "setting" the table, tidying bedrooms, or preparing lamps. Unfinished ironing would usually be done on Tuesday.

All lamps were filled with kerosene, wicks were trimmed, and globes cleaned. None of the lamps were hanging. One, at the entrance to the living room, was kept on a swinging base fastened to the door trim. Others were moved from place to place where needed. In retrospect, it was amazing that none was ever dropped. To have done so would almost certainly have meant the loss of the house to fire. There was no fire equipment within four miles. Open water buckets were always present, but that method may only have made the fire spread. It seems there must have been a guardian angel who prevented it.

The next improvement in lighting was the advent of the gasoline lamp. It had a chrome-like base into which the fuel was poured. There was a valve, through which air was pumped with a small tubular hand pump. A pedestal in the center held the valve, two mantles, and an opaque porcelain shade. The mantle was a small meshwork cloth which, when placed over the flame, gave a white light. They hung on the supply pipe, and when burned became ash-like and were most fragile. These lamps may have been manufactured by various firms, but in this locality Coleman became more-or-less a generic name for gasoline lamps. They were later used as lanterns for camping. We did not have such lamps but rather changed directly from kerosene to electricity later.

All of this has been included to indicate the difficulty of housekeeping. Other facets of it will be dealt with elsewhere. It needs be said here that every family member had daily duties which would change with the stature of the child. No one was exempt. There would, on occasion, be sibling differences which Mom would adjudicate, and from which decision there was no variation. She was fairness personified.

CHAPTER 9

Out Buildings

The large outhouse building stood about fifteen feet from the house and was the first one next to the road, in a row of several buildings mentioned later. It was a two-story affair with vertical siding and no lining or plastering inside. It had four windows downstairs and two upstairs, one on each gable. The roof tapered inside to distance of about two feet at each side, but was about seven feet high in the center. There was a stairway on the left end. It had one entrance on the side next to the house. The floor was about a foot from the ground where a flat stone allowed an easy step to it. Immediately to the left of the door, where one could reach it without entering, was the double-bitted ax. It was never kept anywhere else and had better be there when Dad reached in. Everything had its place.

In the corner beside the ax was a tightly staved barrel without a head. Here was kept dry food for the cow and hogs, and sometimes it even expanded the dog food. This was a ground grain, usually referred to as "chop". A shelf above held a dipper for measuring out the food. In the center of the room was a very plain stove with a smoke pipe that fed through the ceiling to a chimney, supported by the upper floor and a post to the lower floor.

The stove had been a Hathway wood burner which was later replaced by a coal stove. Stored was a large tool box with some carpenter's and general tools, and a smaller box containing masonry tools, those of Dad's trade.

The ever present butcher table had an oak top about three inches thick, eighteen inches wide, and probably six feet long. Near it was a bench with a sausage grinder on one end, and a sausage stuffer/lard press on the other.

The upper floor was given over to a different classification of storage. There were several "dry" barrels filled with beans in the shell, which had been picked from the garden and were drying and awaiting a winter session of bean shelling. This would take place in the evening, and all the family members took part. Beans would be shelled into individual pans or dishes and the hulls periodically burned in the pot belly stove. Not too many could be burned at one time as they were tinder dry and a full chamber of them would make a roaring fire, sometimes burning out excess soot in the chimney and throwing sparks high in the air outside.

Also stored there were tin boxes, most of which had formerly held baker's goods such as ginger snaps, fig newtons, and the like, which had been on display in a grocery. In these were stored a great variety of seeds for garden and flower beds. The containers needed to be mouse proof to keep out a stray mouse before it was trapped or fell prey to a cat, which would be purposely penned in periodically. Cats always stayed in some outbuilding.

Suspended from ropes to the ceiling were burlap bags or sacks filled with other burlap bags, again to avoid damage by mice. A roll or two of binder twine used in shocking grain or corn was also suspended. A grain seeder would also hang. It had a canvas bag for containing the seed. As the sower walked along on prepared soil, he would turn a crank which in turn operated a horizontal wheel. Into the wheel the seed dropped as regulated according to the size of the seed. It was thrown evenly in all directions, giving even coverage. Naturally, some training was required to determine both the speed of cranking and walking. Off season mowing equipment such as scythes, sickles, and grain cradles hung on the walls. A large copper kettle and its stand were kept here and was used in making apple butter. All this is generalization and must not be interpreted to mean there were not other items stored.

The entire building was used for any foul weather repair or

construction work on jobs that could be moved inside. I recall Dad making handles for axes, mattocks, picks, etc., on winter days when a fire would be made in the stove.

Before leaving the thought of construction, I recall that a neighboring friend once framed a backhouse indoors only to find it would not go out the door and had to be torn apart to get it outside. He never lived the story down.

Probably the greatest function performed there was butchering which will be described elsewhere.

At the end of the outhouse and toward the remainder of the buildings was the dog house. The tether of one of the dogs who was at home was long enough to reach the only door into the outhouse. The dog acted as an early security system.

Next, in an easterly direction, were the remainder of the out buildings. The first in the line of these was the "privy," which is described as an "outhouse serving as a toilet." In this family, there was already a designated outhouse. In general use were also other, sometimes vulgar, appellations. The word "general" is used advisedly, since no one was without a back house by whatever name. Ours is remembered for many of its attributes, the most outstanding of which was the seat. It was made of one board which had three graduated openings. Reminiscent of the Goldie Locks story of the three bowls and chairs, the smallest of these openings in this board had in front of it a block of wood for feet which would otherwise not reach the floor.

Floating between these openings would be found a Sears or Montgomery Ward catalogue of some previous vintage, which was there for perusing and using.

Said openings were meticulously cut out, each with a peak on the front side and the whole as smooth as a piece of furniture, unfinished. I recall that, when I graduated to the middle-size opening, I was bitten repeatedly by a spider who lived in a crevice on the underside. Memory does not say how it was obliterated, but it was not to become a permanent fixture. Underneath the board, at a comfortable distance, was a pit in the ground where later a sled-like box was placed. It would be hauled out on the tundra at the farthest corner of the acre lot, and its contents emptied on the frozen ground. By spring it was barely discernible and created no obvious problem.

Once while we were still toddlers, and for no sensible reason, a girl, who was a second cousin, and I threw a cat into the pit. Adults came to the rescue and retrieved and purified the hapless cat. Our punishment is not recalled, but it is certain there was some! It was not the nature of either of us to be cruel in later life, but this must have been done without either of us counting the cost to us, the cat, or the adults. This is among the things in my life I later regretted. Many stories exist relative to someone's backhouse being pushed over, especially during Halloween galas. In our community a lad was peppered with shot for his participation in such a caper. The outcome is not recalled, but there lingers some hazy details of litigation.

In any event, it is likely that someone in your ancestry could, or would have, related tales of interest about a similar necessity. We are inclined to regret the passing of many things common to earlier life style. Need it be said that no one regrets the passing of backhouses or "privies," more so if one thinks in terms of rain, snow, or extreme temperatures. We need to add its passing to the list of the many things for which we are grateful.

The next-in-line building was a slanting roof type shed, nearly evenly partitioned, having two doors on the high front side. The first half was for coal storage. It had a small opening, probably two feet by two feet, with a door opening on the alley side and high enough from the floor so that a full load of coal would store beneath it. The front door was about six feet high, its bottom even with the floor and two steps above ground level. As coal was shoveled in from the alley, boards which were slightly longer than the width of the front door, would be stood on edge inside. As the pile increased in height, another eight or ten inch width of board would be added. As coal was used, the process was reversed.

The other half of the building was for the indoor pigpen and the storage of tools. Tools such as shovels, picks, mattocks, digging bars, and hoes leaned against the front wall. A narrow walk way separated them from a board fence, which contained the two or three hogs in their wood floor area of about ten feet in length. Against the fence was a V-shaped trough for liquid feed or slop. Angled through a crack between fence boards was a smaller flat trough, into which the slop was poured from the safety of the walk, away from eager hogs. Above this fence and about four feet from the floor a corn bin of about forty bushel capacity was heaped with ears.

On the side opposite the coal house was a door large enough to allow passage of the hogs down a stone step to a cement floor. This area was bounded on the east side by the stable wall and on the other two sides by more board fence.

The stable, being about twenty-five by thirty-five feet, was too small to be classified as a barn. The end next to the pigpen had two stalls, two mangers, and a door opening into the alley behind the stalls. In front of the mangers was an aisle from the front door to a ladder leading to the hay mow. The ladder was attached to the rear wall. To the left and inside of the front door was another door which opened into the chicken coop. A cluster of egg-laying nests was attached to the front wall four feet from the floor, with a cat walk for hens to land on when flying up. Roosts made of straight branches and fastened on the walls were on the opposite end. Near the floor was a small opening allowing the chickens out to a slatted pen. As was true of the entire stable, the floor was on the ground.

The hay mow ran the entire length of the building with a door on either side for unloading hay and for ventilation of new mown hay. It was somewhat of a lark and pleasure to sleep overnight there, amid the aroma of the fresh hay. Also, a refreshing nap on a rainy afternoon was one of the country's pure joys.

The roof was covered with asbestos shingles, and in all my years of observation, I never saw a man on the roof as it never needed any care.

Culch

How curious the dialect
That gives us fuzzy words,
So out of ordinary use
Of which we've seldom heard

Stones, old shells, and jetsam
To oyster beds are thrown,
And make a culch in water
Accommodating spawn

So like a cherished by gone pal
Who kept a cluttered bin
Of this and that, most anything
Accumulated in

T'was nuts and bolts, pieces odd
That some would cast away
Were squirreled, cached, or garnered
Against a needful day

Like Edison the wizard
On restless sleepless night,
Searching for a filament
To make electric light

Or our ingenious Maker
From things He conjured forth,
To constitute a planet
We've always known as earth

How fatherly! How caring!
How wonderfully wise!
To make this haven for us
And cover it with skies!

W.K. 12/92

CHAPTER 10

Animals

The first dog I can recall was an Airedale, which is described as "a large terrier having a wiry black and tan coat and a docked tail." He probably seemed to me larger than he really was, owing to my boyish size. He sired Buck and Berry, whose mother is not remembered. Obviously, they were half Airedale and half something else. The mother, indeed, may have belonged to one of Dad's friends. In such a situation the owner of the sire was entitled to the "pick of the litter," and, by some agreement, in this case we got two. I don't recall when or by what means these dogs passed, but later we had a beagle. Sometime later we boarded two dogs for a gentleman who had a country estate. One of these was an English Setter; the other, a half breed Chinese Chow.

Most families had at least one dog, some would have fox hounds or coon hounds, and there was no dog food at the store. They would be fed table scraps, sour milk, and sometimes a grain mixture flavored with something like "cracklins," a fat residue with the lard pressed out. They might be fed offal from beef, pork, or fowl, generally cooked outdoors in an iron kettle. Sometimes there would be surplus buttermilk, or bonny clabber, which was milk which had become thick in souring. No by-product went to waste. If meat was bought at a butcher shop, the butcher would donate from his bone pile for the dogs.

If a farmer had a sick or injured animal, he would sometimes notify some of the dog owners. If the animal were ambulatory, it would be led to a wooded area and be afforded a mercy killing. Even if the animal had died rather than been killed, it would be dragged in the snow or hauled to a woods, and dog owners would simply turn their dogs loose until, with the aid of some scavengers, the carcass disappeared. The adage which says that "nothing is to be gained by burying a dead horse" is true. Unless the animal had been a family pet, few were buried. In later years, and to this day, carcasses are hauled to a rendering plant. In the wild, scavengers only need compete with each other. The dust-to-dust law of nature prevails some way.

We usually had only one cat at a time, but if it were a female who was free to roam, kittens would appear and must be given away or destroyed at a very early age.

When our family was larger, three piglets would be acquired early in the year from a farmer who had good stock. Immediately, they would be force fed. Ear corn would be fed twice a day and slop at least once. This would be, basically, ground grain scalded with boiling water, sometimes a bit of powdered stock food, and any of the aforementioned by-products available. On occasions, dish water would be added and the mixture stirred with a paddle and poured into the described trough. Gluttony, increased by competition, caused the disappearance of the food in jig time.

Men in the village who raised hogs vied with each other to raise the largest hog by butchering time. Dad spent some leisure leaning over the fence at the outer pen and made a clicking sound. The pigs would come, and he scratched them with a stick, which they seemed to love. He would also throw in a shovel of coal, which they loved to chew and eat, a shovel of dirt from the garden, or a chunk of sod. Potato peels or vegetable trimmings, if not fed to the cow or chickens, were also fed to the pigs. Nothing digestible went to waste.

Since the pigs were on a wood or cement floor, they were always relatively clean. Anyway, they had rings fastened in their noses to prevent their rooting—even at the fence. They are rooters by nature. Also they made their toilet on the farthest corner and avoided that area except for that purpose. On Saturdays, whenever the necessity arose, a lad would appear in boots and with a scoop shovel to throw the waste, empty corn cobs, and soiled straw bedding over the fence into the alley.

There were never more than two cows. By the time I was big enough to handle a cow, there was only one. She was tied to the manger with a three-strand chain, one of which had a swiveled T fastened at its end. The T was pushed through a hole in the manger and the other two met and fastened at the top of the neck. In winter she was more or less a prisoner unless there was no snow or ice on the ground, in which case, she may be lead to water at a small stream close by. In this stage she was like a bed-fast patient. Her food consisted of hay, corn fodder, some dry food (at milking time) with apple or potato parings, or chopped pumpkins in season. Here again, it would occasionally be sprin-kled with purchased stock food. Water would be carried from the well in buckets, and in extremely cold weather would have hot water added. Droppings and soiled straw bedding would be thrown out the back door onto the manure pile. Mom milked the cow morning and evening, insisting that anyone else would spoil the cow. Always the milking was done by hand, from the same side. The pail would be carried to the cellar. On the way a por-tion of the warm milk would be poured in the cat's pan. In the cellar it would be put through a strainer and cheese cloth into a crock. Overnight, the cream would rise to the top to be skimmed off the next day and held in a cream crock to await churning every few days. This would be done with a vertical stomper churn. When butter rose to the top in small granules, it would be taken out, rinsed in cold water in a wooden butter bowl, salted lightly, and patted into a mold. The skim milk in the crock could be used for cooking, and any surplus fed to animals, as the but-termilk from the churn could also be used.

Just after a calf had been born, a cow would give the most milk. The calf would feed at the udder when very small, then weaned, and fed some milk while graduating to solid food. After months of milking, the cow would gradually go dry and soon be ready for breeding. At that time, by prior arrangement with a farmer who kept a breeding bull, a boy would be delegated to lead her there and back. She was led with a four or five foot length of clothes line with a loop on one end. This would be thrown over the neck and the other end put through the loop, which was drawn up loosely along the side of the neck. Another loop was formed by doubling the rope, giving it two twists, forming a third loop, which was put over the nose. The end of the rope was the rein. This halter-like system was adequate to control the cow even if she were frightened or just frolicsome.

All summer long she was led to pasture each morning. I recall two pastures which Dad had rented on different summers. One of them was a good long country mile away, and on the way back home was a blacksmith shop, where I would stop and watch the smithy, Herman Knupp. He might be shoeing a horse, sharpening tools, or fashioning some iron object. To heat the metal on his open furnace, he turned a crank on the bellows with his right hand while poking coal with his left. The iron to be shaped was put in the bed of coals with tongs, heated until red hot, and then moved to the anvil to be shaped by his hammer.

Before nailing a shoe on the horse's hoof, trimming of the hoof was necessary. The odor produced by the cutting was a most unusual one, unlike any other scent—not objectionable, simply unique.

Time flies when something fascinating is happening, and sometimes I would be tardy getting to some task to be performed that day. Before sundown, a return trip had to be made to bring the cow home for milking and resting overnight. Sometimes she would be waiting at the gate, and other days she would be lurking in some far corner of the pasture, necessitating a search. If flies were particularly annoying, she might hide amid the thickest, brushiest spot where she could brush them off. She didn't always come if called. Her name was Lady, but, at times, that was a misnomer.

For chickens, we always had Rhode Island Reds. Some people kept White Leghorns, which were reputed to be better layers, but they were small and slender. Reds made bigger and better roast chicken and layed dark eggs, which some cooks declared were better.

They needed to be fed morning and evening. The principal fare was shelled corn and, sometimes, wheat. Being penned up, they had to be supplied with "scratch" in the form of crushed egg shells, or in a slow laying season, ground oyster shells which were bought. These were necessary for grinding the food in the gizzard—characteristic of fowls. Water was usually kept in a shallow, wooden bucket which had originally come from market, containing salted fish, and was sealed with a wooden top. With the top off, water could be reached by the chickens standing on the ground, and it was not easy to upset. If ice formed in winter, it would be melted with warm water.

Our baby chicks were hatched by a clucking hen. In spring, egg laying diminished and a number of hens would sit on empty nests, or perhaps one with only a glass nest egg in it, and she would acquire a mean attitude. They would make a clucking growl and peck at any hand that disturbed them to check on the nest. Under one such hen, we would put a dozen eggs which were marked all over with a pencil, hedging against the rare chance that a laying hen might deposit a fresh egg, while the nesting hen may be off the nest for food or water. As the chicks were hatched, one or two at a time, they were taken out of the nest and kept covered in a box or basket, usually behind the kitchen range. When the full clutch had arrived, mother and chicks would be put in an "A" shaped pen, one side of which would be covered with galvanized tin, the other side and ends were slatted, allowing the peeps to get in and out. The mother could only get her head out to call and scold as the situation demanded. As the chicks grew and became feathered, the mother would again join the adult flock. The pen would be propped up to allow the larger poults access, and a roost would be added. When they became a hazard to the garden, they would be joined to the adult flock.

Chickens were not allowed to range free. They could devastate a garden, and always defiled a lawn and walkways with droppings. Sometime, just before dusk, they would be freed to run and fly for exercise. Perhaps animals, like humans, need some diversion to remain healthy.

Sometimes in summer, egg production diminished and there would be only one egg to "gather." My hands being occupied otherwise, I once put the egg in my pocket and forgot it. Life's experiences are incomplete without having a broken egg in one's pocket!

CHAPTER 11

Butchering

Depending on the size of the family to be fed and the number of hogs raised, one or more fall days were set aside for butchering. When the older children were still at home, all hands were on deck and assigned to sundry duties. When they grew up, they sometimes returned with a spouse to assist. It seemed to me that Frank and I, being the youngest, assisted for many years—as long as we lived at home. Thanksgiving was a favored day as most of the married siblings were free from jobs and the gathering evolved into a work of sociability.

The preparatory work was, of course, done in advance. An open-end barrel was kept for the purpose of scalding. Its bottom was set a-tilt in the ground, backed against the coal house and leaning onto a platform supported with low wooden horses and a board platform. Two iron kettles supported by three legged rings were set about a foot off the ground. A supply of wood was on hand and kindling for starting fires. The large table, made of one wide oak plank about three inches thick, was a permanent item in the outhouse where the processing would take place. The table was five feet long. A sturdy bench had a meat grinder attached on one end, a sausage stuffer/lard press on the other. One sat on the bench between these for ballast while turning either crank. Several knives, along with a sharpening steel and a cleaver, were also standard, along with a hand held meat saw. All of this had to be washed. Since it was cold weather, fuel had to be gathered for a coal stove on which an ancient iron tea kettle full of water rested. Large pans and tubs were available for throwing lean trimmings and diced fat for making lard. These were conveniently kept under the large table.

Butchering day began before daylight when we boys would make the fires under the water-filled kettles and stoke them until the water boiled. When this happened, it was time for the starting gun in the form of a 25 caliber rifle which had been "freshed out" from a rusty 22 caliber, but it still shot a rim fire cartridge. It would be aimed at the upper forehead of the pig and was usually effective. When the pig fell it was stuck with a long knife into the lower end of the throat, where it reached the heart causing the carcass to bleed out as the animal kicked its last.

Once while we were camping in the Pennsylvania North Woods, the old resident on the farm where our camp was located requested help to hang up a hog. His method was to stun the hog with a large wooden potato stomper-like implement, which he wielded from standing at the hog's side. It immediately fell, and he quickly stuck it as described earlier.

In case there are some squeamish readers, they are referred to chapter one of Genesis where God instructed man to have dominion over fish, fowl, and cattle. The tenth chapter of Acts tells of Peter, being in a trance, hearing a voice saying, "Rise, Peter! Kill and eat." From a standpoint of practicality, one could not butcher a live animal.

Having now a dead hog, and a barrel half filled with nearly boiling water, a member of the crew set a long heavy sharp steel hook, having a looped handle, into the roof of the hog's mouth. It was dragged to the platform and dipped into, and out of, the hot water. When the hair began to loosen, the carcass was reversed, and with smaller hooks was hooked through tendons in the back of the hind feet. The head end was dipped. If the hog was large, it may have become necessary to lay burlap on the midsection and pour on boiling water. When all the hair was loose, it was removed with a hollow disc scraper which had a handle mounted on the convex side.

A three legged pole hanger, bolted loosely at one end, was laid on the ground with the two outside legs on one side of the bolt, and the center leg swung over to the other. Between the outside legs the carcass was laid and the tendons of the hind feet attached to iron pins in the hanger. The bolted end was raised and the hog hung on a tripod. The carcass was washed and readied for the next operation.

The head, now hanging downward, was cut off next to the shoulder. Then the abdomen was opened from neck to tail and the entrails dropped into a tub to be dealt with later. A cut was made on both sides of the backbone and the ribs sawed from it. Now there were two halves and a strip of backbone, which was taken to the bench where the skin and under layer of fat was removed, and the spine sectioned to be ready later to cook with sauerkraut.

Then, one-half of the remainder was taken to the bench where ham, shoulder, and flitch (for bacon) were separated, trimmed, and set aside. Lean trimmings would be later ground for sausage meat and fat rendered for lard. The other half was treated in the same way. The head was trimmed, the snout, skin, ears, lungs, and other scraps cooked for dog food later. The lean trimmings were cooked for pudding meat.

Then the entrails would be dealt with by removing the liver and heart for pudding meat. The large intestine was scraped of contents, washed, and

Brother Alfred "Butchering Day"

soaked in salt water to be used later for sausage casings. Parts of entrails not usable for dog food were buried or taken to the woods for wild creatures to love or leave.

The two iron kettles come into play again. The smaller one was now used to cook the pudding meat. When cooked, it would be put through the grinder and returned to the kettle into the broth, with possibly a little water added. Now corn meal was added. While being stirred with a wooden handle, the meat and meal would cook. When the mixture reached a semi-liquid consistency, it would be ladled into bread pans. The end product is known today as scrapple, but at the time of this described activity, it was referred to as Pannhaas, a word of German or Dutch derivation found in a Pennsylvania-German dictionary.

The larger kettle was then fired and the cubes of fat were put in it for rendering. This took considerable time and needed regular stirring to avoid sticking. The paddle used had originally been made for an axe handle, but was relegated to this job because of its wide, paddle-like end. When the cubes had shrunk and turned a tannish-brown, the kettle was lifted with a pole through its bail and was carried into the outhouse to be ladled into the presser. As the lid was wound down on it, the hot liquid ran out a spout at the bottom and into a fifty pound lard tin. This container had to be placed in a partially filled tub of cold water until the contents cooled, otherwise the hot liquid would melt its seams.

Overages would be put into crocks of one or two gallon size. The fat was compressed into a ring of "cracklings" about one inch thick. Some people liked to nibble on these out-of-hand. Others baked them into corn bread or stuffings. At our house, they were usually used to flavor dog food.

Whenever it was convenient, the lean trimmings were ground and pressed in the same apparatus used for the lard, with the inner colander-like strainer being removed. The clean casings were stripped over a longer spout and filled with sausage, some of which would later be canned in glass jars. These were usually two quart size.

The hams, shoulder, and flitches would either be dry salted or covered with salt brine strong enough to float an egg. When "cured" they would be threaded with binder twine for hanging in a smokehouse. Uncle Cicero had a smokehouse where he kept a smoldering fire of apple or hickory wood. I can't recall how many times it was my duty to haul them on a wheelbarrow the quarter mile or so away. On the maiden trips they would be protected by a large sheet. On the return, they would be in flour sacks with the twine exposed. They were then hung in the outhouse and taken down for slicing as needed. In the bags, they would keep for many months.

This was a busy time for every one. Dad supervised in the outhouse, and Mom, with help from a daughter or two, was busy preparing for canning, planning, and cooking a noon day meal for all hands. She also had to determine what could be kept for early use. This would include pork chops, backbone, sausage, and scrapple, none of which could be kept too long unless it happened to be freezing weather. A great deal of this sort of thing would be given to the helpers. Sadly enough, after working with the stuff all day, it would take a couple days for the keen appetite to reappear.

In any event, we had plenty of pork requiring no cash outlay. Sometimes, Dad would go to town on Saturday and return with a beef roast or a bucket of salt mackerel. Along about February, when most were "porked out," some farmer would butcher a beef and Dad would buy a quarter, usually the less costly front one. As written elsewhere, we always had chickens on which to fall back. We were never without food, as were some folk in those days, although it was somewhat of a "meat and potatoes" diet. Even the stores did not have the varieties known in later years, and in our case, the only refrigeration was the cellar.

The "Village" of Waterford: 1) The Homestead, 2) The 3 room schoolhouse, 3) Christian Church, 4) Brethren Church, 5) United Brethren Church, 6) Rehm's Store, 7) Brother Alfred's Store

Author, older brother Frank and "Zeb"

A few "Fine Men" at Rehm's Store, circa 1918

"Fashions" of the 20's

Dad, Duggan Robb, Author and Frank with their "turtle catch"

Four sisters, 1-r: Myrtle, Estella, Jean and Anna

"Barefoot" Author Wade Jr.

Our barber, "Bill" Knupp and wife Hattie

Dad with the "Boys," l-r: Ford, Frank, Author, Alfred and Glenn

Mom with the "Girls," l-r: Estella, Myrtle, Anna and Margaret

Dad with a few Grandchildren

More Grandchildren

By the old Grindstone, l-r: Author, Dad, Frank, Glenn, Ford and Alfred

l-r: Glenn, Frank, Alfred, Ford, Dad and Author

l-r: Margaret, Anna, Mom, Myrtle and Estella

At left, 3 steps up to the "Powder Room," out building at right showing a few of Mom's flowers

Dad at the barn with "Community" deer hides

Just before Army induction, Dad and Author "cradled oats"

"Harvest Time" Author & Dad in Fall of '43

Dad and Mom 1943

"The Boys" at Hunting Camp, l-r: Author Wade, Frank, Glenn, Ford & Alfred

Mom and Dad on their 60th Anniversary

Kinsey Family Museum in Waterford, Open to the Public

CHAPTER 12

Bereavement

Although reluctant to write this chapter, I remember it as a part of the way life was. It would be unfair not to write of it.

All human beings experience bereavement at some time, if not many times, in life. Anguish is felt in a secondary way when someone in the community suffers a loss. There is a sympathy which seems to flow toward those who are beset with misfortune of any kind. Probably the most bitter wound to the spirit is usually suffered by family members through the loss of a loved one to death. As noted elsewhere, our parents suffered the loss of five children, four of whom died at very early ages. The fifth one was, age wise, in the middle of the family and, therefore, intimately known by all.

Willa Jean, who died in 1925, was 15 years old. She died as the result of peritonitis following an operation for a ruptured appendix. She had been adjudged by the family, her school mates, and anyone who knew her, as the fairest and most likable of the entire family. Only recently, a neighbor of that day spoke of precisely what has just been written. More could be said about the specifics of her personality, but the previous statement seems all embracing. The shock of the loss was as sudden as her illness was brief. Antibiotics were unknown.

Dad, who was not one to demonstrate his emotions, was visibly broken. He was pacing on the lawn when the long-time pastor approached him. Dad had never shown partiality to any of his children, but he was aware of the general fondness for Jean. He inquired as to why she must be the one to be taken, even though he, nor any other parent, would have wanted to chose another. The pastor pointed to a blooming rose bush and remarked that anyone plucking a rose would select the most perfect flower, suggesting that God may have had a better plan for this flower.

Mom was the most cruelly touched of all. From what I can remember, she made every effort to console everyone else. Frank and I, being eleven and nine years old respectively, tried to comfort her with the thought that Jean was now in heaven. Her reply was, "Yes, and I want you to be good and meet her there."

In those days viewing was held in the home. All of us who lived there went in and out of the house by way of the kitchen door. The front door to the living room had no steps outside. A neighbor, who was a carpenter, came immediately and built steps. Neighbors brought food and performed any other helpful acts they could think to do. I don't recall the individuals involved, but neighbor men would have automatically dug the grave. All of this sort of help was customary community practice.

On the night before the funeral, after callers had left, Frank and I stood before the casket on the way to bed. We each held in our hands our shoes and black above-the-knee stockings, trying to console each other. The next day, I stood on the lawn and watched the casket being placed in the hearse. When the funeral director closed the door, the latch made a piercing sound which I have never forgotten. The service was held in the church, which was filled.

At the cemetery, the scene was typical of the time. The pile of freshly dug earth was plainly visible and held in place on the side next to the grave by a series of old fence rails. There were no vaults, and the plain, unfinished "rough box" was visible, the lid laid atop the pile of earth. There was also no lowering device, but two rails were across the open grave, upon which the casket would be set for the grave side service. At the conclusion, pall bearers placed straps beneath the casket, removed the rails, and lowered it into the rough box. The service ended. It was the practice that some folks would take a choice flower or two from the offering.

Life must go on. Grieving would continue and become exceedingly painful at the time of the next rainfall.

All of this would seem to become totally devastating, except for the hope of heaven which was embraced by the mourners.

Particularly, to assuage Mom's grief, our brother Ford, who lived in Ligonier, brought a radio and a series of wet batteries, as electricity had not yet been made available. It would be difficult to measure the success of the venture, but the effort was commendable.

I recall that later in the summer the World Series was being played, and the radio was moved to the front steps. It seems there was no other radio in the village, and since the weather was favorable, the baseball fans gathered on the lawn. They were able to hear a description of the game in which Pittsburgh won the pennant (1925).

CHAPTER 13

Health

Except for the death of our sister Jean and the infants, the remainder of the family was blessedly healthy. We had the usual childhood diseases which were not followed by serious after effects. No one had the slightest deformity. All were active and capable. We did endure a couple of cases of scarlet fever, but had no experience with typhoid fever, which claimed perhaps three people by death in the community. Generally speaking, it seemed the population took health for granted. Physiology was taught in the upper grades of school, but there was not the media exposure we were later to know.

To the extent that we were equipped for cleanliness, it was practiced. Mom was, to a marked degree, careful in storage, handling, and preparation of food, considering the fact that the only refrigeration was on the cellar floor.

Dishes were washed without benefit of hot running water, and automatic dishwashers hadn't even been seen in the imagination. Our dishwashers were girls of varying ages who had to be tall enough to reach over the top of the dry sink. There were stories told about punishment because the dishes were not done at the appointed time. The water would have been heated on the coal range as has been discussed elsewhere. The dishwater had to be thrown outside, generally on the garden, as there were no drains in the house.

Bathing was also not done in the manner of later years. In winter, it was done in the living room beside the coal heating stove described elsewhere. People scoff at the idea of the "Saturday bath," but it was the typical pattern of that day. If the bather were big enough, he or she carried in a galvanized tub, set it beside the stove, and carried warm water to fill it. Privacy was always respected, except in the case of small fry. Daily washing was done in a basin and involved only the "high spots" and exposed areas. If there was some special occasion, midweek bathing could be done. Previous generations bathed mostly with homemade soap consisting of used fat and lye. We had graduated to "Ivory," "Fels Naptha," and "Octagon" which was used for harsher jobs. No one gave the matter much thought as it was common practice. Some families may have had a spring/gravity fed supply water, but in most cases it provided only a single tap at a kitchen sink. Indoor plumbing was available only in towns with city water.

The common cold was a general nuisance, but considering the fact that people were exposed to the elements more, it did not exist in epidemic proportions. One wonders why this is so, in view of some of the existing practices such as the common drinking dipper both in school and at home. When a cold was contracted, several stand-by cures were used, Vick's Vapor Rub and Camphor were the most commonly used for exterior treatment; however, not the only ones. These products were rubbed on the chest generously, and in case of a head cold, Vicks was put into the nostrils. Although the instructions advised against it, some people swallowed it. Mustard plasters were also used on the chest area depending on the severity of the illness. In cases of small children, raw onion juice and sugar were given internally. There is an age-old argument as to whether colds are caught because of exposure to bacteria. If the medical profession can't cure the common cold, how could a writer be expected to know all the answers?

One thing is known about colds, in those days paper tissues may have been in existence somewhere, but not at that time and place. One carried a cotton handkerchief or cloth, which proved at times to be woefully inadequate.

Earache was more common with some children than others.

Warm sweet oil would sometimes be poured into the ear. I recall that my father would blow pipe smoke in my aching ear and plug it with cotton. I remember one family in which the eardrums erupted, and this condition was referred to as bealed ears. It always seemed that it would be spelled that way. It could not be found in any of three dictionaries, so it must have been colloquial.

The daily brushing of teeth was not a common practice until later in my youth. That the older siblings had some natural teeth all of their lives was fortunate and unexplainable. Aching baby teeth were simply pulled. Mom, understandably, lost most of her upper teeth in mid-life, and my older brother, Alfred, bought dentures for her while he was yet unmarried. For cuts and abrasions there were many remedies, such as peroxide, iodine, and assorted salves. Some of these still exist. I recall White Cloverine, Rose Bud, and Porter's Pain King. There were no Band Aids, but if covering was indicated, white cloth and adhesive tape were used. Anyone knowingly exposed to poison ivy would wash at earliest opportunity with strong soap such as Octagon or Fels Naptha. If this did not help and blisters and itch appeared, Dad had on hand liquid sugar-of-lead. He and I were both susceptible. I itched in the most unusual places, and that medication felt like liquid fire. I was once told of screaming so as to be heard two hundred yards distant upon the application.

There were, of course, herbs and teas for a plethora of ills, description of which would fill volumes. A couple of the most common, used externally, were lamb's ear and milk weed, juices of which had curative powers. Plantain leaves were used for bee stings. Vinegar, ammonia, and other readily available liquids were used for some problems.

In my family history, four generations before me, two boys in one family died in a small pox epidemic and others with diphtheria. My younger brother died at age one in a flu epidemic. An elderly man recently told me he had been vaccinated by having a cut made on his skin, and a scab from another child who had been vaccinated was placed in the incision—it "took." During the early part of the century, children died of what was diagnosed as "summer complaint," since doctors were not privy to information or some medication later known.

All of the foregoing was to indicate that today's family has many advantages for which they are not appropriately grateful.

Since there was no indoor plumbing, waste vessels were provided for nighttime use. There were what were referred to as "slop jars," which were probably ten or twelve quart in capacity, galvanized, having a flared top, a bail, and a lid with a handle. There were also porcelain chamber pots of smaller capacity with lid and handle on the side. All vessels were naturally carried to the toilet, dumped, washed, and returned each morning. In case of diarrhea, the victim would go by lantern light to the toilet, weather notwithstanding.

Since bedtime is in mind, it is appropriate to mention mattresses. Early on, they were composed of straw, packed into blue and white striped ticking. They were hoved up in the center until in use for a night or two. After a time, the straw settled and formed to fit the bodies. Periodically, it was necessary for the girls to rearrange the straw and turn the mattresses.

In summary, the general good health which the family enjoyed was, like the success of the gardening, attributable to Providence, genes, and nature.

CHAPTER 14

School

The school to which I went was, in the beginning, a two-room building with a hallway between rooms. Sometime during the years I went there, it was converted into a three-room facility, including the former hallway which was of no practical value. Probably this measure was taken to avoid building a separate, more costly unit. In the two-room plan, grades from one to four were in the "little" room, and five to eight in the "big" room.

Because I had opportunity to talk with Mattie Tissue, (later Mattie Noel), who was my teacher in third grade, special attention is paid to that year. Since I began school at the age of five, it would be 1923. My brother Frank was two years older, but was only one grade ahead of me in school. I always used this as an excuse for my lesser scholastic standing but learned, as I grew, to know the truth! The teacher was paid forty-five dollars monthly for nine months.

Miss Tissue had lived in Oak Grove, half the distance between Waterford, where the school was located, and Ligonier, where she had gone to high school and to a "normal" school in summer. She walked to both places. Although she had to walk to teach in the winter, she had only leather shoes without Arctics (galoshes). Roads were not routinely plowed, and snow was sometimes deep. Sometimes, she would have arranged with one of the larger boys to build a fire early and have the building warm for the younger children. It was her responsibility to build and keep fires, as well as to furnish kindling.

The school directors would have provided the coal in an outside coal house. A local farmer or trucker would haul it and shovel it into the bin for three to five cents a bushel. It would have come from a "custom coal" mine. These were small operations which were sometimes run as an adjunct to farming. The stove was a large pot belly with stove pipe going up through the attic, because the stove needed to be in the center of the room. Around three sides of the stove stood a frame the height of the stove, which was covered with galvanized metal sheet to prevent students from touching the stove. Underneath, the floor was covered with sheet metal to prevent hot cinders from reaching the wood floor. Flooring was narrow pine tongue. It was oiled each fall with kerosene. Of course, the coal had to be carried in and the ashes carried out. The walls had only clapboard outside; inside was a beaded sort of wainscoat nailed horizontally to the wall. The ceiling was of the same material with no insulation between the board layers. It was generally either too hot or too cold. Hooks were spaced along the walls for hanging coats.

Windows were generously spaced along side walls and were covered with heavy metal screening. There was no insulation. The sash was of medium size panes, probably for safety reasons. There was only one doorway leading to the hall. It was placed near the outer wall, and the remainder of the front wall was covered with blackboard. A trough below it held erasers and chalk. In most rooms pictures of Lincoln and Washington adorned the wall, along with an American flag. A large-faced pendulum clock, probably a Sessions or Seth Thomas, was also present. The teacher would sit between the desk and blackboard, facing the pupils, of course! In front of the desk was a long recitation bench where an entire class would sit for oral examinations. The day began with a reading from the Bible, saying the Lord's Prayer, saluting the flag, and singing a patriotic song.

Desks were double, usually shared by pupils of the same grade, with larger ones in the rear. The sloping desk had a sunken ink well and underneath was a shelf for books. The seats were hinged and raised when not occupied. There was a groove near the top of the slope for pencils and nib pens. The front of each desk held the seat for the next one.

There was a fifteen minute recess mid-morning and afternoon. During this time, pupils could go to the toilets which were located behind the school and separated as far as was practical. Each sat over a pit and had a blind built in front of the door side. Outdoor games such as overball, tag, baseball, and races were played.

Overball was played with a rubber ball. One team would stand on one side of the building and throw the ball over the roof of the school to the other side. If someone caught it, he or she would run around the school and hit a member of the other team, and take a prisoner. Eventually, the better team would have all the members.

By fall, grass would be growing on the school yard. It could not survive long, and the area became a sea of mud. In winter, if snow covered the ground, a "fox and geese" ring would be made with spokes leading to the safe harbor in the center. Someone was appointed "it," and needed to catch someone else out of the safe center and exchange places. Girls sometimes played indoor games such as jacks.

When the teacher rang the bell, recess was over, all too soon. As the students gathered on the porch, a couple of brooms were provided for sweeping off mud or snow.

Obviously, this hurry-up job was not very successful, and mud and water always accumulated under the seats. Early birds would have time to get a drink at the water bucket in the hallway where a long handled dipper floated. All drank from the same dipper and lived! There was little or no hand washing, and most of the pupils carried lunch pails. We who lived close enough could hurry home for lunch.

Health care supplies may have included a bottle of iodine and a box of salve. There were no Band-Aids and no paper tissues. Colds sometimes affected many of the pupils at once. Some parents had their children wear a cloth bag filled with assafetida—a foul smelling chemical (as the name would imply). This was supposed to ward off germs, not to mention the wearer's companions.

Water came from a drilled well, over which was a cement

platform and an iron pump. Volunteer students most times carried coal, water, and ashes, or stayed after school to help sweep out the mud or dust chalk erasers. This practice was not frowned upon.

The proverbial "hickory stick" of song was really more likely to be in the form of a sturdy paddle. The teacher wielded it to the posterior while the offender lay on his or her anterior on the recitation bench. This was generally accepted as having been "just dues." In case of rebellion by the pupil, the parents could be summoned, or indeed the offender could be expelled from school. It was quite a common practice, if the parents were informed of a punishment, for them to administer a repetition at home—just to assure that the message got through. Rarely was there any defense by anyone.

On Friday afternoons, before dismissal, there was usually a period reserved for pleasure, sometimes taking the form of reading of a continued story by the teacher. One such story mentioned was "Secret Garden," or some favorite of the pupils. There may also be poetry reading or singing. This may have been an attempt to set the stage for a pleasant, well deserved weekend for pupils and teacher alike.

For the most part, once the teacher got her supplies for the year, he or she was very much left to personal ingenuity. There was a county superintendent of schools, a position held for years by Professor Charles Maxwell. He would come, unannounced, once or twice per term of nine months. The teaching of penmanship was, for years, under the direction of the P.O. Peterson Method, from which directions came by mail and occasionally a visit from the system.

Periodically, if the supply of any material was depleted by midterm, it was the teacher's responsibility to acquire the same at a central supply in Ligonier, four miles distant.

For holidays, especially Thanksgiving and Christmas, extra effort was made to produce appropriate art work. For this the system provided mostly yellow and white construction paper. If memory serves correctly, crayons would have been brought from the homes when available. The results may have been more primitive than I remember, but it was the beginning of a new interest and allowed for some anticipation in an otherwise rather routine existence.

The teacher was at once the instructor, disciplinarian, confessor, cajoler, encourager of art and music, nurse, custodian, and above all else, the example and mentor. As a rule, the position was highly regarded by all in the community. In later years, many pupils were to return with gratitude and praise for early instructors.

It has long been argued that children in lower grades learned a great deal by being exposed to the instructions for the higher grades in the one or two room schools. It seems to be generally accepted that, in addition to the three R's, earlier schools also afforded social interchange not then available by many other means. It perhaps revealed actions not necessarily evident in their own closely knit families. It must have molded character, as generally shown in society of those days.

It would seem appropriate to touch briefly on the high school experience of that day. The school was four miles away. Buses were unheard of, and few families of that time would even consider taking students to high school, even if they had the means to do so. Dad never owned a car. Some students, particularly the girls, boarded in town and went home only on weekends. The standard practice was walking. Sometimes a commuter would pick up students.

For a considerable time Frank and I rode in an open truck with a heavy wire cage on the sides of the bed. The owner, Mr. George Riffle, hauled milk to the creamery. He visited farms by a staggered route which considerably extended mileage. At each farm we would unload the empty five or ten gallon cans for a particular farm and load the filled cans. A full ten gallon can was quite heavy. By comparison, ten gallons of water would weigh 80 pounds— plus the weight of the metal can. Each seller had his own number painted on the cans. In severely cold weather, it seemed a long way to town. Evenings we walked or hitch-hiked home.

For two or more of the five winter span covered, we were the only two students from our village to attend high school. We carried lunch in paper bags, and the boys ate in the furnace room of the three-story combination elementary and high school building. For the first couple of years, we were the "country kids," and were joined by those from all over the township.

The town students were acquainted as they had gone through grade school together. Additionally, they had a different life style as their homes had city water, electricity, gas, and indoor plumbing. In most cases, there were few if any chores to be done and more time could be spent at homework. By the second or third year, we became acquainted and integrated, except for extra curricular or social life. It had to be conceded that, for many reasons, the town groups were a generation advanced in life style. By junior and senior years, we were quite well adjusted and may even have joined one of the cliques.

The three-room school

CHAPTER 15

Cobbler Shop

My grandfather had been a cobbler, one who could not only repair shoes but also could cut and assemble a new pair. His son, Cicero, learned the trade from his father, and after his father's death continued the business for the remainder of his life. The shop was located at the lower end of the village and about half the distance to a grist mill toward the west. Once when I was a preschooler, Dad was taking grain to be ground and took me along. It was probably the last winter before I entered school, and I would have been the only child in the house during the day. Hence, my delight in the trip. Since there was snow on the ground, Dad hauled the bags of grain and me on a homemade sled, which was almost three feet wide and had wooden runners.

The mill was modern enough to have mechanical grinders, as opposed to older millstones, but it was still operated by water power. Its location was higher than the main stream so that a breastworks was built on a bend up stream, and a nearly level mill race carried sufficient flow to operate a water wheel and power the grinder. The water was returned to the main stream via a "tail race." I seem to remember that we were taking shelled corn to be ground into meal and placed in heavy paper bags, because it would sift through the coarser bag in which the corn was brought. We also seemed to have brought oats or wheat to be ground into chop or middling for feeding stock. As I understood it, oats ground into chop and middling were made up of oats with bran from wheat or rye added. I could stand corrected regarding the formula, but in any event, both were fed to stock.

The mill was an old wooden building which seemed to me to vibrate excessively when the grinder was running. Due to lack of exercise enroute, I was probably chilled. In any case, the place was cold, and I was happy to start the return trip, as on the way we would stop at the cobbler shop and get warm during the visit. The shop was divided into two rooms, the back one of which held supplies and was closed off. The front room had a pot belly stove in front of which stood a wooden box partially filled with ashes which served as a cuspidor. Men congregated there, some of whom were bringing or taking shoes. Others were simply there for sociability and discussions of affairs of the day and politics—always politics. No one, save the cobbler, was there when we arrived.

Uncle Cicero sat on a low cobbler's bench which held wooden pegs, nails, flax cord, bees wax, hammers, awls, and knives. He could reach the floor for shoes and leather. He usually had a lap iron on his thighs where he could cut out thin leathers for uppers, tongues, and patches, and also shape heavier leather with a hammer. The iron was a rectangular metal piece, probably one-by-eight-by-twelve inches in size. Thicker leather for soles

The Old Mill

was soaked in a bucket of water which was always black, apparently a residue of the bark used in tanning. Though he had a sewing machine for thin leather, he sewed the soles laboriously, a stitch at a time, with what were called wax ends. These were made of the flax cord with a bristle twisted onto each end. The cord would be waxed with beeswax. A groove would be cut near the edge of each piece of heavy leather, placed back-to-back. In the groove, a hole would be punched with an awl from one groove to the other. Then a bristled end would be pushed through from each side and drawn tight—one stitch. Hard wood pins were also sometimes used in soles—presumably as an adjunct to wax ends.

By this time in history, bartering was practically ended and business was mostly on a cash basis. There must have been, however, those who did not pay upon delivery of the mended shoes. On the wall behind the stove there was a rather crude picture of a beagle dog with its feet in the air and a caption which read "Poor trust is dead! Bad pay killed him!" How effective it was is a matter of conjecture, as the results were never discussed.

Outside the door there hung a silhouette of a calf-length black boot of wood with the lettering "C.L. Kinsey." This was much like the twisting design at the barber shop, indicating the type of business conducted inside. Inside of the cobbler shop was the perpetual odor of leather which was as unique as that of the blacksmith shop, or the luscious wafting from a bakery. All of this was intriguing to a small boy and still is in the memory of an old man.

Uncle Cicero liked to have a pet dog in the shop, and at one time had one who must have annoyed someone in the neighborhood. There was an oft told tale that the dog was rubbed under the tail with a corn cob, and a liberal dose of turpentine was applied. One can only imagine the explosive action of the dog and the rancor that existed between the owner and perpetrator, though his identity was not immediately discovered.

Another "dog tale" evolved when a dog named Tippy followed Cicero's son, Wilson, to school and must have been distracting or frightening the children. The teacher ordered the boy to send the dog home which he tried to do without success. Finally, in desperation, he yelled "Go home, you son-of-a-bitch." The teacher made ready to administer a paddling when she suddenly realized the injustice of such action. While the language was uncouth, it was also a true utterance, and the case was dropped. Perhaps the incident was concluded with the ringing of the assembly bell.

There was always a rocking chair in the cobbler shop where one could sit comfortably and watch the cobbler deftly rejuvenate a much-worn shoe, though it always irritated him when the repair had been delayed too long, as it made the repair more difficult. Once when my brother Glenn took such a pair for repairs, our uncle, the cobbler, grumbled about Glenn's delay in bringing them for repairs. Glenn retorted that the shoes could be taken to Ligonier where there were two able first generation Italian—Americans, either of who would be happy to repair them. The cobbler recanted and agreed to the repairs. In spite of this encounter, they were best of friends until the demise of our uncle.

Now let us regress in time to this cobbler's father who preceded Cicero in the shop and from whom the trade was learned. He was Henry Kinsey II, born in 1832 and died in 1896. He was the third generation descended from Jacob Kintzy, who homesteaded in Bedford County, Pennsylvania. Two histories have been written about the family, and a museum to its memory and honor stands in the village of which you have read, Waterford. That, however, is quite another story and is not to be dwelt upon here.

Henry II operated the shop, the time span of which is not positively known by the writer. It was, of course, an even more primitive operation than Uncle Cicero's. Word of mouth indicated that he was known to have, on occasion, carried a side or pelt of leather for great distances, probably from Greensburg or Johnstown. His business was largely on a bartering basis, and his "day book" is still in existence. He had a son-in-law, William Weimer, who lived next door. An effort will be made here to reproduce pages of his day book, showing an account of the bartering.

Granddad not only repaired shoes but could make a pair of boots "from the ground up." These were calf length, and many of them were made on a straight last. They were called "straights." Different opinions have been expressed as to how they were worn, one being that they could be worn on either foot and were worn alternately to avoid uneven wear. Another supposition is that even though made over a straight last, they could take the shape of either foot. This was said to have been made easier by thoroughly soaking the boots early in the day and wearing them until dry. Leather soles would become exceedingly slippery, especially when one was walking on dry leaves or grass. This could be overcome by wetting the soles.

Dad told me that proud owners sometimes had "screechers" built into the soles by having the cobbler place the smooth side of the leather next to the rough side. The smooth side came from the exterior of the animal's skin, the rough from the interior.

Most shoe leather was cowhide. Placing the screecher was generally done with fine shoes which could be highly polished and were worn for dress shoes. There was vanity in those days, too, apparently!

Before leaving the subject of shoes, let me mention an item related to me by my Dad, which his brother-in-law, William N. Weimer, acted out! In the fall of the year, he cut a small branch to the foot length of each of his children. These he carried over the mountain to Johnstown, about twenty miles distant, where he measured and bought shoes for all. Then he carried them back home in a burlap bag.

The reproductions from Henry Kinsey's day book are included to emphasize the extent of bartering that was in effect during the latter part of the 19th century.

Individual accounts are shown to illustrate the variety of items traded.

6

William Welchons A D 1887

July	2	To mending per of Shoes	8 5	
Oct	6	to by three Bushell Corn ears		60
Nov	3	by ten Bushell nubens corn		1 20
Dec	10	To mending glass	5 0	
	11	To mending Bridel	1 0	
	13	To mending per of Shoes	7 0	
	12	to by one Bushell turnips		50
March	2	To mending Bridel A D 1888	2 0	
		to by halling hay from Tashes		1 50
June	11	To mending harness & shoes	7 5	
	21	To mind gears	2 5	
	15	To mend shoes per wife	4 0	
	21	To mending one Shoe per self	8 5	
Nov	24	To mend gears	3 0	
		to by halling corn foder from Clarks		1 00
		A D 1889		
	28	To mending Roof & Bridel rain	4 5	
	4	to by halling hay from Tashes		1 25
		to by ten duck Eggs		15
May	22	To mend per of Book	8 0	
July	6	To mending per of shoes wife	3 5	
		to one halter	5 0	
		to one per shoe string	0 5	
Oct	17	to by Halling corn from Clarks		1 25
	18	To mind shoes	6 5	
Nov	25	to by halling hay from Jones		1 25
Dec	12	To mending gate latch	0 6	
		to by halling seed corn		1 00

Barefoot

Time of winter on the wing
   Giving way to signs of spring,
Warmer days the spirits thrill
   Nights of Arctic breezes, still
Time for cold to lose its sting.

Youngsters tired of winter's grasp
   Yearn for brighter days at last,
Weary of the indoors pent
   Long and stagnant hours spent,
Hoping nature's sleep is past.

Yawning, slow the summer wakes
   Sunny skies upon the make
Full of playful outdoor cheer,
   Neighborhood companions near
Work and play their hours take.

One of summer's choicest joys
   For the country girls and boys,
Waiting for the cheerful news
   They could shed the winter shoes,
Freedom for the bare-foot days

But the ground is frosty still
   From the evening's stubborn chill,
In a distant carving low
   Can be seen a drift of snow
Over on McKelvey's Hill.

Finally, the happy day
   Now the snow has gone away,
And the father gives the news
   "Kids may go without their shoes."
Bare-foot time is here to stay!

Now the soles become quite tough
   Treading o'er the region rough,
With its stubble, briar, and stone
   Till the tenderness is gone,
Rather like a horse's hoof

In the puddled places low
   Oozing up between the toes,
Mixed of earth and summer rain
   One of childhood's pleasures plain,
Scene on scene adventures grow.

Or perchance a gurgling stream
   Wading through a toy boat dream,
Catching, freeing crabs or newts
   'Neath the sunken stones and roots,
Time's forever!—so it seems

But alas! The season wanes
   Easy duty, now begins,
Pulling weeds or stacking wood
   Teaching habits useful, good,
Gentle prodding showing gains

Then, the tiresome evening wash
  Time consuming, slightly harsh,
Dirty feet and up to head
  Clean, before it drops in bed,
Dreamland in a hurried dash.

Interest now in new shoes showing
  See how fast the feet are growing!
Comes the plan to winterize
  All those feet in larger size,
Broken in before the snowing

Cycled life in stages racing
  Youth and age together pacing,
One day, pain transgresses pleasures
  Life doles out in varied measures,
Fearless ones go wisely facing

This the stuff of memories making
  Good and bad their places taking,
Our times have their ebb and flow
  Such is being—here below,
Then, into the future breaking

W.K. 1992

Through the Cracks

He lived in a tumble-down shanty
    Across from the oil well dry,
His pleasures seemed notably scanty
    As seen by a quiet passer-by.

Trudging his way to the store
    Whenever his larder was bare,
T'was a high-light to ride in a car
    When a driver was willing to share.

His chewing tobacco was habit
    Even while riding he sat,
And if the occasion would have it
    He'd spit in his grimy old hat.

Alec's Abode

He'd labor back up to his burrow,
    To his humble lair unkept
With dishwashing left for the morrow,
    And seldom the floor would be swept.

To the lads in the village t'was sporting
    With "spirits" consumed—and in hand,
To Alec, a toast, while cavorting
    With laughter and jokes a la grand.

The host would then graciously offer
    Fried eggs, bread, and butter with jam,
A treat which the lads wouldn't suffer
    Preferring to tend toward the "lam."

For the cat was asleep in the skillet
    A-top of the rusty old range
With eggs, Alec planned he would fill it
    As the cat quickly opted for change.

But the lads had politely declined it
    —The treat that was on Alec's mind,
And they'd oft in the future relate it
    The generous gesture—and kind!

The place of his youth was a mystery
    He likely of kin was bereft,
Naught could be told of his history
    And few were aware when he left.

W.K. 2/93

CHAPTER 16

Churches

In earlier times the church was not only the fountain of religious doctrine, but also the center of social life. There was no other entity which gave opportunity to gather three or more times weekly. I am reluctant to even mention the word gossip, but in truth, no other contact gave occasion to spread even the best of news. There were three churches in the village, all of whose bells could be identified by anyone within listening distance. In order not to show partiality, they will be listed in order of their distance from our home.

The nearest was the Church of the Brethren which was little more than the length of a football field away. Beyond it, but a short distance, was the Christian Church. In the opposite direction along the same main road, and less than a quarter mile away, was the United Brethren Church. Each of these was housed in a single room rectangular, wooden structure with a raised platform in one end where stood the pulpit. Sunday School classes were gathered in little clusters. One or possibly two of the buildings had an excavated area underneath where a hot air furnace fed one large floor register. The third church almost certainly had a pot belly stove. Each had an upright piano to assist in unified singing. All were lighted by kerosene lights, and each had one segregated outdoor toilet.

The basic beliefs of Christianity were common to all; all accepted the Bible as the inspired word of God. The King James Version was the popular choice. In retrospect, it appears that they agreed on the principal tenets of Christianity far more than was generally acknowledged in the early part of the century. The early ecumenical movement seemed only to be whispered in the higher echelons of the Church. There were, however, not so subtle differences in the practice of certain traditions. Without becoming deeply involved in beliefs of sacred matter, perhaps we may consider some of the differences of opinion among the local denominations.

The Church of the Brethren has as their creed only the New Testament. They believed in nonviolence, temperance, and the practice of religion in life. Their baptism is performed by immersion, placing the body forward in water three times. They have a regular observance of communion and an occasional love feast, in which they serve a symbolic lamb stew and wash each others feet. They subscribe to an over body, which fact would classify them as a connectional church.

The Christian Church also claims its creed in the New Testament, and aims to restore the New Testament Church in its doctrine, ordinances, and living. It is also known as the Church of Christ. They commune weekly and baptize by immersion, placing the body backwards under water one time. They have only a loosely connected affiliation with a Sunday School Association. This is the church to which our entire family belonged.

In both of the mentioned instances, the baptisms were performed in a clean flowing stream or pond, and often during winter weather. They have a sort of pride in the trust that no one will, or has suffered any physical hurt from the practice. Many, if not most, of the churches who practice immersion now have indoor baptisteries under controlled conditions. Also in these fellowships, membership in the body and taking of communion are preceded by baptism.

The United Brethren Church began during the latter part of the 1700's. They experienced a revival movement in Pennsylvania, Maryland, Virginia, and later spread westward. They merged first with the Evangelical Church, and later with United Methodist Church. At the time of which this writing depicts, they were classed as United Brethren, and a portion of the congregations still are. They claim always to have been Evangelical in practice, and to be classified between Protestant Fundamentalists and Liberals. They practiced the sacraments of communion and baptism, but did not agree with the practice of only one method of baptism. They allowed sprinkling, pouring, and immersion.

In all of these churches was the practice of holding revivals, or "big meetings," usually in winter. I think it needs to be said that there was great effort at persuasion, but also a measure of "hell fire and brimstone" crept in. In any event, these meetings produced repentance, conversion, and baptism through which the membership expanded. They also sometimes produced long-winded evangelists who would remind a listener of stories similar to the one recently appearing in a church bulletin:

"Last Sunday, the Preacher just kept on preachin' and preachin' and preachin'. Finally I stood up, picked up my coat and hat, and started walking toward the door. Preacher asked, 'Where are you going?' 'Preacher,' I said, 'I'm going home to mow my hay.' He asked, 'If the hay is so important to you, why didn't you mow it before you came to church?' I said, 'When I left to come to church, it didn't need mowing!'"

The Christian Church—rear portion is the old church moved from another location.

United Brethren Church.

Brethren Church of today.

Paragon

A sprightly wisp of lady
I met when just a child,
With graying hair already
And manner sweet and mild.

In rustic church, her teaching
To children round her knees
Whose eager minds are reaching
For visions that she sees.

Tales from holy writ she took
And passed to minds like these.
And, from a colored linen book
She taught our A B C"s.

These matters later helpful
For living, on the whole,
Providing mettle useful
For body and for soul.

Her kind had a mission
— Enhance the human race!
May others learn devotion
To rise and take her place.

W.K. 2/93

CHAPTER 17

The Mail Man

One of the vivid memories of childhood is that of the mailman. During the span of my life at home only one man served the rural route, of which there were two, out of Ligonier where the post office was then located. Before my time there was a post office at the village of Waterford, which was earlier called Boucher, as there was a larger town by the name of Waterford, and the state could not have two offices by the same name. Also before my time, a man by the name of Harry Stom carried mail on horseback, as the volume was low. He had a dog which always followed him, and so the story was told, ran the route alone on Sundays and holidays.

The only carrier I ever knew was Russell Betz. He always had a buggy, as volume was heavier, and he delivered parcels, newspapers, and even baby chicks in springtime. His buggy was drawn by two horses. It was a rather square, high thing with a windshield in the front and sliding windows on each side, even though the mail was delivered to boxes on the right side, except in rare cases. Slots were cut under the front window for the two horse reins. Behind the seat was another sliding door leading to a compartment where parcels and bundled mail could be stored. He had two horses who ran at a trot between deliveries and had learned where each stop was to be made. In addition to deliveries, he sold stamps, envelopes, and took applications for money orders, which were written at the office and delivered the following day. He also collected money for C.O.D.'s. When someone came out for a transaction, the horses waited patiently and started out only when he made a clicking sound with his tongue.

He was on somewhat of a schedule and arrived at our house about noon, six days weekly. Folks knew about the time of his arrival and often waited for him, as his time was precious. In summer the horses were annoyed by flies, and he, by heat. He naturally carried his lunch.

He lived in Ligonier. His sons would help tend the horses. I don't know if they harnessed them in the morning, but they certainly would unharness at night. The horses needed to be curried and brushed each evening, fed hay and grain, and watered. Harness was hung on a rack at night, bridle removed, and halter put on. In winter the harness always had a string of bells when the sleigh was used. Before he left the office in the morning, it was his duty to sort the mail into pigeon holes in the order in which it would be delivered, and bundle it with straps. His route was number two, and was principally north and east of town.

I am not aware of the number of families served, but especially in winter, he would not return until dusk or later. Winter was entirely different and more difficult. The enclosed buggy would be a blessing, and he had a foot warmer of some sort in the bottom of it. There was little attempt at snow plowing, and that was done by farmers with teams and pointed triangular drags. At times, it simply got too deep, and the horses would be belly deep in snow. In certain areas that were prone to deep drifting, the men in the area would volunteer to shovel out the drifts, and, depending on the next snow fall and wind, might find it filled again the next day. There were heavier snows at that time.

I recall that during my very early school days, we walked on a crust over a three foot paling fence in our yard. At such times, Mr. Betz would go as far as possible sometimes leaving the road to take to fields, where the snow had not drifted as much. At times, he had to retrace and start out again on a different road reaching as many families as he could and retracing again. Of course, not all of the route could be served in this way, and if the snow prevailed he would have a backlog of mail, the remainder of which he would have to recase at night to have it in sequence the next day. Also, sometimes people who had not been served would call at the office for their mail the next morning while he was casing a new shipment.

He rented stalls for his horses in the Weller barn which stood between North Market Street and North St. Clair Street. A man who lived in the era related the following story: One of the horses he had was a bay mare. When she came in heat, some of his "friends" had her bred without his knowledge. I was not told about the outcome of this prank. Without intending to be harmful, people in those days were not above perpetrating tricks on each other. Humor was not as evident in those times, and the results of some practical (and impractical) jokes were grist for story telling far into the future.

At a later date, when a farmer drew up before a general store, the driver dismounted and entered the store. In his absence a young lad pulled the "linch pin," which connected the double tree to the wagon tongue. When the driver remounted and called to the horse to "get up," they started to walk away from the wagon. This resulted in no real harm as the team could only go a couple of steps until restrained by stay chains attached to the front of the wagon tongue. None-the-less, it would be told half a century later. Indeed it was told to me.

Mr. Betz's son, Glenn, related to me that part of the mail route included a stretch of somewhat primary road which was still unpaved, but had enough auto traffic to cut deep ruts. These would have been made by contemporary cars, mostly Model "T" Fords, which had high spoke wheels raising the body above the depth of the ruts. The buggy wheels would follow the ruts where the horses trod the higher ground. To the driver, this gave the appearance of being pulled up hill.

The carrier furnished his own equipment. When he began the job, he was paid $30.00 a month. He retired in 1945 at the age of 64 after 35 years of service. He lived to age 84 on a pension of $2200.00 per year. His was a somewhat coveted job in those days. He had steady income, no layoffs, and security, so long as he performed his job well, and so long as the United States Government prevailed.

That he performed well was attested to by the fact that he was beloved by those whom he served. He was an even tempered man of integrity and, incidentally, a very devout churchman. His son related that each fall for many years, Mr. Betz and a couple of other men bought hogs at three or four cents a pound, butchered, and processed them into marketable products. These were sold for the benefit of his church, and the proceeds used for satisfying current needs of whatever sort. It is presumed this would have been done on some of his personal vacation time.

His duties were not always performed without difficulty, but he obviously persevered. His determination was typical in those days. A man found his greatest help at the end of his own arm. Generally, he had family and friends to give him succor in time of misfortune, and there was a very personal concern for others. Relief, however, came in the form of empathy on the part of charity of friends and neighbors. This sort was a personal affair, which began to evaporate to a great extent with the beginning of public assistance. There was an adage in both business and organizations which said, in effect, "what is everybody's business becomes nobody's business."

A typical Mail Buggy, not Mr. Betz.

CHAPTER 18

Coal Mining

Although my father, and several members and in-laws of my family, worked at times in mines, most of my knowledge of it was only recently acquired. George "Kelly" Thomas, who at age 88 is still married to my only surviving sister, Estella, recently talked at length to me about mining. His experience was varied, but most of it was spent with Baton Coal Company who had a mine at Wilpen, Pennsylvania. It is a small town whose name is a contraction for William Penn.

Even the transportation to work, a distance of about four miles, could be considered a saga of its own. Early on, it was provided with a Model "T" Ford. Before the times of electric starters, the motor had to be cranked by hand. The crank protruded in front of the radiator. Sometime when the gas in the motor first ignited, the crank would "kick" backwards with force enough to break an arm. In winter when the motor oil became stiff, cranking was most difficult. In the coldest of times, the oil would sometimes be drained and heated on the coal range overnight and poured into the cold motor in the morning. If the motor were one which started only with difficulty, there was yet another tactic possible. If one rear wheel was jacked up and the emergency brake put in the high gear position, when the crank was pulled, the wheel spun. This centrifugal force would sometimes cause the motor to catch on and run. Early Model "T's" had only curtains, and this era predated heaters. It was cold! On the return trip, leaving the warmth of a mine in sweaty clothes and riding home was quite a shock.

In 1926 Kelly worked in the coke yard which was, of course, outside. In 1927 he began his time inside the mine. He was teamed with Bill Kissell, and they both loaded the same wagon of coal onto which they hung a brass token stamped with their number. This identified their work when it was dumped from the tipple onto a railroad car. The wagon of coal was pulled out of the mine on a track by a gasoline motor.

Now let us try to determine how the coal gets from the vein into the wagon. Even though this is bituminous, or soft coal, it is very hard as found in the vein. It has been formed under tremendous pressure. It is described as "coal that yields pitch or tar when it burns," as opposed to anthracite or hard coal which gives much heat and little smoke. In this locale, the veins are usually six feet high; whereas in some areas, the vein is eighteen to twenty-some inches high and must be dug by a miner who reclined on his side to mine and load the coal. Standard equipment for those miners was heavy knee and elbow pads.

In the higher veins, to get the coal down off the "face", the miner must mine by hand at floor level an area of probably twelve to fourteen inches high and likely the same distance into the "face". This is done by use of a "pick" which is a mattock-like tool having two very pointed ends. There is a knack for digging coal loose in a low position, but even after the knack was mastered, it is the hardest kind of labor imaginable. When the coal is taken out of this area, an auger is used to bore a hole in the face high above. The resulting hole is of a circumference to barely allow a half stick of dynamite and cap to be tamped in, and to allow wires to lead out for conducting an electrical charge to set off the cap and explode the dynamite. From a successful charge the coal on the face will fall down in manageable chunks and finer pieces, ready to be shoveled onto the wagon. Short handled shovels with a twelve or fourteen inch wide scoop were used. A veteran miner once stated that the secret of success was in making sure the scoop was full each time it was raised. I have no written record of the number of wagons loaded each day, but it seems to have been in the order of eight or ten wagons at two and a half ton each.

For this work each miner furnished his own tools. This included pick and shovel, a carbide lamp which fit on the cap, carbide and container for same, pole ax with a blunt edge for driving wedges, and a long auger.

The carbide container was a flat metal box which would fit in a pocket and had a sliding lid on the end. The lamp had a water container at the top and water dripped onto the carbide to form the burning gas. A regulator on top determined the drip. If the light dimmed, more water was needed. Periodically, new carbide was added.

A charge was made for sharpening a pick, dynamite, and shot caps. When hard hats eventually became available, each man bought his own. Each man earned two dollars and fifty cents per day which for a twelve day pay netted $30.00. At this time, Kelly was paying $12.00 monthly for rent. Sometime during his early experience as a miner he bought a used Ford Roadster for $125.00.

In early days the miners were responsible to throw aside the "gob", a chunk containing slate which occasionally showed up. When the "face" was moved back, a cross bar of timber was set up to hold the roof, and was supported on each end by a wood post. The timber had to be wedged tightly against the roof, hence the pole ax mentioned earlier.

Some employees lived in company houses and bought at the company stores. If buying had been excessive, at times deductions exceeded pay. Neither of the men mentioned above lived in the immediate vicinity and bought little, if any, at the company store.

The sequence of events is not certain, but apparently by 1933 the owners proposed a company union, which was not accepted and a strike ensued. During this time, Kelly went to work in the pickling shed of Latrobe Steel Company Mill. He had taken the physical examination and bought new shoes, overshoes, and overalls. In a month the soles dropped off his shoes from the acid used in "pickling" steel to cleanse it of rust and other impurities before processing. Clothing also had holes burned into it. At this plant, Sam Bills, the husband of another of my sisters, Myrtle, also worked. He retired from it years later. He lost the third finger of his right hand due to an infection from a sliver of steel. He was also hospitalized at one time having had his feet burned by the acid.

In a short while the United Mine Workers Union was voted in, wages increased, and working conditions changed for the better. It is not known by me whether the unionization caused the change, but in 1934 cutting and loading machines were installed. Kelly returned to the mine and ran the cutting machine. His former partner worked on the loading machine, and Glenn "Shupe" Kinsey, Kelly's brother-in-law, ran the scraper which took the coal away from the cutter. Once, the cutting machine hit a hard area, which they called a sulfur ball, and threw the cutter off track and cut Shupe's foot badly. Though he had to be taken for immediate medical treatment, his concern was that a new boot had been ruined. He was never allowed to forget the unlikely concern. On another occasion he was caught between two cars on an inside curve, and his spine and pelvic area were crushed. He lay in a body cast for weeks having been told he would probably never be able to work again in masonry and in building contracting. This prediction was later to be proven false.

Kelly worked at that mine until it closed in 1945. Not only was the work hazardous, but very dirty. Daily bathing was tedious and time consuming—no quick showers to hop into. Injury could come as it might in any employment, but there was added risk of being caught in a "fall" from the roof. The air could become contaminated by "Black Damp", a suffocating gas which was a mixture of carbon monoxide and nitrogen. Fresh air had to be pumped in through overhead shafts. Movement of the air in the lower temperature of the mine felt quite cold to the men when they stopped work to eat. Safety lamps which would go out in the presence of hazardous gas were used for periodic checking of air quality.

"Custom" coal usually was furnished by small mines scattered over farm areas. Often these would be operated by one or two men to furnish coal for local domestic use. The digging was done in much the same manner, but the loaded wagons were drawn by mules or Shetland ponies, or indeed, pushed out by man power.

The coal was hauled to homes either by truck or horse teams and shoveled into the coal house, or basement, by hand.

Years later the government subsidized payments to victims of "Black Lung" disease brought on by long term breathing of coal dust.

There was a camaraderie among miners as among any other group. There were also sad and devastating occurrences when one nearby was seriously injured or killed. Often a fellow worker was relegated to go inform the family of the calamity. Doubtless there were other jobs done elsewhere in the successive chain of the industrial age which were difficult, but it would be hard to imagine one more dangerous than coal mining.

After the interview with Kelly, which was the source of most of this information, his son later told of seeing his dad come home from work after having twisted his back. He climbed the cellar stairs on hands and knees, but with home treatment and rest, insisted he was well enough to return to work the next day. Necessity seemed to demand it. He went.

CHAPTER 19

Outdoor Sports

There were few men in the village who did not hunt, especially in their formative days. Of course as a boy, one could improvise a gun, interchangeable between shotgun or rifle types, according to the game being played. Small fry looked forward anxiously to the day when they could hunt, which was, at that time, age sixteen. In the meantime, they looked with envy as older brothers or fathers emptied their game bags or brought home a deer.

The deer were mostly bucks, and the degree of pride which one showed was determined by the number of points or tines on its antlers. Doe seasons were not opened every year, but when they were, the men would gather in a group and have a "drive". A certain area would be hunted with part of the group stationed as drivers and the remainder as watchers. If there was a doe season declared, it was because the herd was too numerous for the food supply in the area, and was usually allowed on a county-by-county basis.

One year during the time when I was quite a young hunter, two men, Bert Jones and Charley Houpt, owned trucks and took them for hauling the deer. By evening, as I recall, there were probably twelve or more deer in each truck. They were carried or dragged to the parking place, where a tag was required for each deer specifying the successful hunter, the hour killed, caliber of rifle, and date. A game protector was often a member of the group.

Even in time of deep snow, if the herd were not oversized, the deer would gather. This would usually be near a stream; often numbers of them were found dead of starvation. Deer are naturally browsing animals, but if the browse was out of reach, they would convert to grazing. In deep snow, grazing was impossible. For these reasons, timbered over areas with lots of new ground growth harbored a lot of deer.

Each family was responsible for dressing and cutting into meal-size portions their own deer. In freezing weather, the venison could be hung in an outbuilding and eaten gradually. In warmer weather, it became necessary to can the meat in a cooked state, usually in one or two quart jars. Jerky could be made, but that was not a common practice, as smoking was a long process for so small a quantity. If no family member were adept at processing the carcass, a friend or neighbor usually assisted. Incidentally, in a short time, any dog in the neighborhood could be seen with a deer bone or even a head. Hides could be sold for tanning. Books could be written, and indeed have been, about deer hunting.

Just prior to my hunting days, my brother Glenn had an excellent hunting bitch, which was half beagle and half Red Bone. She had been bred to a beagle, which combination indicated likely wonderful trailers for rabbits. Glenn, who was my instructor in matters of the outdoors, promised to give me the pick of the litter when the puppies arrived. This much anticipated event occurred in May. My choice was a male beagle who was white with reddish tan spots. Even at his young age, I had trained him to run rabbits by fall. I was still one year away from hunting age. Dad suggested he be named Peco. Since I didn't want an ordinary name for him, I agreed.

His reputation as a good rabbit dog became common knowledge among the hunting fraternity. I had two people offer me $25.00 for him. Now at this time, $25.00 was practically a fortune, but not enough to buy Peco. I refused the offers. One night many dogs in the village disappeared. A day or two later all had returned except Peco. I was never to know what happened to him.

Peco's grandmother, whence he got his Red Bone heritage, was better at night hunting for possum, coon, or (unfortunately) skunk. Her owner, Bert Jones, was a generous man who would allow us to take her on night hunts when we were too young to hunt small game. She was too old to cope with a fast and smart old coon. Never-the-less, especially on a damp night, she would tree a possum which we could shoot down with a .22 caliber rifle. We never questioned whether the practice was valid, nor did anyone else.

Small game season was also much anticipated and usually began on November first. Rabbits, squirrel, grouse, and ring neck pheasants were legal game. Rabbits were pursued vigorously and were kicked out of creek banks, brush piles, hollow logs, or sitting atop the ground in a cozy indentation in grass or leaves. If an open hay or clover field were hunted, the method was to zig-zag sharply as you could walk by without disturbing the quarry. Much effort was expended in those days. More modern Nimrods rely on dogs for routing, or simply walk in a straight line. Four rabbits constituted a legal bag.

Ring neck pheasants preferred corn fields, fence rows, or heavy cover such as clover or alfalfa. Usually shot on the wing, they were an elusive target, and in most cases the two limit bag was appreciated, if acquired. Ruffed grouse were woodland dwellers. It seemed the thicker the growth, the better for them. The bullet speed and noisy flush caught hunters off guard, and a two limit bag was even more appreciated. People who were strictly bird hunters liked to have a Pointer or Setter dog which would point, hold, and retrieve. Few people in the village were such specialists, and to this day, I never hunted behind a bird dog.

Squirrel hunting was a less vigorous sport as one could sit and wait in a woods which had good feed and nesting. One could also walk slowly and quietly and come upon them. Grey squirrels were most widely shot. Red squirrels were shot out of contempt. They were predators to other small game and birds. They also had the unsavory reputation of castrating grey squirrels. The bag limit of combined squirrels was six.

Glenn, whose nickname was Shupe, was my sponsor and mentor. When I began to hunt, he loaned me a double barrel shotgun with a trade name of Plymouth, which I think may have been manufactured for Sears. Glenn, meanwhile, carried a Marshwood, possibly from the same source. He was my personal safety course. I later suspected he had acquired the Plymouth for my benefit. Later, when I was earning some money, he sold it to me for the grand sum of $15.00. We became quite a team, and a rabbit routed between us had little chance to escape. Some of my most pleasant memories are of hunting and camping with him. This does not mean that I neglected hunting with my other brothers at some stage. All of them are remembered fondly.

Like everything else that came into possession of our family, no game went to waste (nor to waist either, I might add). One of the early rules of the sport was that every hunter cleaned his own catch. Rabbits were generally fried, squirrels made into a delicious pot pie, and birds were usually baked.

An incident only obliquely related to hunting comes to mind. Once, when Frank and I were preschoolers, Dad was going to the woods and wished to take the mixed Airedale/hound dogs. He instructed Frank to feed and water them first. In the process, the dogs jumped to get the food before it was poured and Frank kicked one of them just as Dad approached. Knowing he was in disfavor, Frank ran into the outhouse and squirmed himself into one of the oven doors which opened on either side of an old cook stove used there. Thus hidden, he was nowhere to be seen. Dad left for the woods, and by evening, no mention was made of the incident. Frank later became a medical doctor, and I have wondered what would have gone through the minds of some of his patients could they have envisioned their trusted physician ensconced in an old oven.

Later in my hunting experiences I was to come by another shotgun. Earlier in Dad's life, he had acquired a double-barreled gun made by Ithica. All of his friends who smoked saved tobacco tags to add to his collection. I regret to say I never knew the tradename of the tobacco. Anyway, the gun was offered for a certain number of tags, and that's how he came to have a new hunting piece. As I was named for him, he promised me at an early age that I would inherit the piece which he nicknamed, "Old Ironsides." He had ordered it to his own specifications. As stated elsewhere, he was blind in his right eye, and therefore shot cross-fire, and had the open and choke barrels reversed. As promised, he did give it to me when it was apparent he would no longer use it. I have used it since, allowing for the reversed barrels. It is still in my possession.

Though it happened before my time, an incident was related to me. When there were still wild turkeys in the area, Dad killed one. There were also chestnuts maturing, which the turkey had just eaten and which had not yet reached the digestive tract, but were still in the brown shell, stored whole in the crop. They were washed, and apparently the children were allowed to eat them. Later when he was leaving to hunt, Myrtle said, "Dad, get another one of those big birds with the chestnuts in it."

Playing somewhat second fiddle to hunting was fishing. In that locale, trout fishing was the principal pursuit. Mill Creek, a fresh water stream, was favored as the place to catch large trout. It ran the two miles to Oak Grove before being polluted with sulphur water from mine drainage. It had some quite large pools which would produce sizable brown trout, but they were temperamental and seemed to only feed when they were ready, rather than when the fishermen were there.

The stream had three tributaries in the mountain, sufficiently pristine for brook trout to spawn and produce native fish. Brookies seemed always to be feeding and were more readily caught. When first caught, they had a most beautiful array of colors, which would fade when exposed to the air. Most fishing was done with earthworms, which were generally spaded out in the garden and carried with a little soil in a tin tobacco can having air holes. If the water was high and roily, a lead sinker was attached above the hook.

Before my time there was a creel limit of twenty-five fish per day, and the legal size was six inches. By my time, the size limit still prevailed, but the creel limit was reduced to ten fish. As fishing pressure increased, size was increased and limits decreased.

In warm weather, fish were carried in a creel and packed in wet sweet fern. Tackle consisted of an inexpensive steel rod, reel, and line. Not much attention was paid to leader material, but most hooks had a six or eight inch gut snell.

Fishing differed from hunting in that the catch did not have to be cleaned in the evening when one was already weary. Trout would be cleaned on the stream, and except for a cold rinsing, would be ready for cooking. They were always fried.

Since there were no bass lakes in the area, the only other fishing generally took place in the slower and warmer water of the meadow streams. Suckers were more difficult to catch on a hook, unless one stood for a long time waiting for them to nibble at the bait. They were more easily caught with a loop of fine stiff wire attached to the end of a heavier wooden pole. The loop would be slipped gingerly over the fish's tail and, about mid-body, would be jerked tight. It was called a "dull," which name was of dubious origin and is not found in the dictionary. It was none-the-less in common usage and readily understood. The practice was frowned upon by the fish commission and was ultimately outlawed, probably before we practiced it. Since suckers are very bony, they are more or less considered junk fish, even though the flesh is good, unless taken out of a stale muddy pond.

Another practice, which had essentially died out before my time, was that of "gigging." This was done with a four or five pronged metal piece, the rear end of which was driven into the end of a long handle or pole. Tines on the front end were flattened to points and the entire apparatus was used to spear fish or frogs. A gigging party consisted of three or more men, at least two of whom carried kerosene torches to show light on the quarry. Though it was outlawed before my day, I recall seeing a gig hanging along a rafter in our outbuilding.

To be successful, this method of taking fish or frogs would have required some practice because of the refraction of light. When the handle was partly submerged and passed from the medium of air to the medium of water, the point of impact was not precisely where it appeared to be. An allowance had to be made.

Now please consider an entirely different method of capturing a quarry. Some people catch turtles by using a large, baited turtle hook. It is secured by wire to a stake or root. The bait can consist of any kind of refuse flesh, either from trimmings or internal organs. A turtle will impale itself on the hook by snapping at the bait. More recently, the wire could be fastened to an empty, sealed gallon size plastic jug. A turtle being hooked to this arrangement finds it impossible to submerge and keep the jug under water because of the heavy pull on the float. Therefore, it will stay near the surface. Often it is necessary to have a boat to recover the trap and quarry. This is considered by most people to be a cruel method, which was rarely employed in my time and never by an old-fashioned turtle fisherman.

Their method was to wade in a stream, reaching under roots or any other recess where a turtle would be resting, head first, during daylight hours. By feel, one could identify the shell, tail, or leg of a sleeping turtle. One of the secrets of the method was that, having found such prey, one never let go to give it a chance to reverse ends, and turn the biting end out. Generally these were snapping turtles, but occasionally one found a less ferocious terrapin type known as a "red leg." Either was edible, but the latter was more difficult to prepare for cooking. Once caught, they were placed in a burlap bag and given to the "sack bearer," of which there was one or more in every party. With a half dozen or so turtles in the bag, it became cumbersome and heavy, and carriers either spelled each other off, or had another bag into which to split the load.

The fourth of July was a traditional turtle day since most people were on holiday and help was available. The bearers also carried the personal items of the fisherman. This may include wallet, pen knife, tobacco, and, depending on who was fishing, possibly some sort of liquid "nerve" medicine. The oldest clothing was worn, because of the risk of tearing it to shreds. Though it was rare for anyone to be seriously cut or injured, sometimes broken glass or other sharp objects would be felt. Non-poisonous water snakes were always present but were eager to get away. The only things Dad ever was cautious about, were muskrats. Turtles were not averse to stopping in their underwater holes, and a rat could bite before one was aware of its presence.

I digress to say, once, after Dad had died, Shupe and I decided to go for turtles. Only one nephew was along for carrying the bag and moving up the vehicle along an adjacent road. We were going upstream, Shupe on one bank side, and I on the other. I heard him cry out, and looking around I saw only a big spot of blood from a rat bite. It had nicked an artery on his wrist. We immediately left for the hospital while I pressured the cut with paper towels, until he insisted on temporary relief and the process began again. By the time we arrived at the small hospital, the bleeding had stopped. It being the fourth of July, there was no doctor on duty. The nurse, after cleaning the area, called the doctor who prescribed a tetanus shot, but Shupe was allergic to tetanus. The doctor agreed to a half shot of a human derivative medication, which was the only action required. This was only one of many such instances in his life, as he was quite accident prone.

Turtle Hunt "catch of the day" Brother Glenn with a 19 pounder, Grandson Kurt and neighbor Jimmy Rote

We return to continue the turtle fishing tale. Once when we were on a certain stream, our older brother Alfred, the prankster, was along. He lagged behind while others fished through a rough stretch having overhanging thorn trees, logs, and other flotsam. He left the stream and found his way to a bridge ahead. When we came into view, having had no success, he came off the bridge to a very easy access open area, and with little effort pulled out a fairly large turtle, a typical performance.

When the fishing concluded and we returned home, it was customary to dump the catch out for the benefit of the group gathered. The turtles would then be put in a headless barrel kept for the purpose, and into which had been poured a few inches of water. There would be much snapping at each other until they settled down and apparently went to sleep again. Boys would go hunting for crabs to feed to those who were not soon taken out and cleaned. The cleaning process began by having a bucket of scalding water on hand. Then the turtle would be taken out and placed on its back. They had a way of extending their necks, placing their heads on the ground, and turning over. When the one to be cleaned put his head on the ground, he would be snatched by the head so that his mouth was held shut. Being thus rendered harmless, the head could be pulled out and severed with a sharp knife. The severed head will still bite or snap onto an object. When it stopped kicking, the turtle was immersed in the hot water, after which the skin could be peeled off and the thin plastic-like squares taken off the shell. It was then cut along the under side of the shell, which lifts off the body with only the neck attached. The heart would still be beating. The entrails would be removed and buried. No domestic animal will eat them. The toes would be cut off with a cleaver. Both sections would be boiled until the meat, of which there are seven varieties or colors, comes off the bone easily. It was then ground and added to vegetable soup, which Mom had made in large quantities from garden fresh vegetables. Sometimes, more than one turtle was required. Company often came, usually an in-law family. The soup composed the entire meal. It was served with soda crackers, or homemade bread and butter. Celery salt was a favored additive.

My Dad told me about the worst whipping he ever got. He was quite small when one of his older brothers was cleaning a turtle, and he snapped the severed head on a cat's tail. As the cat circled the house, his father administered the whipping.

When time permitted, aside from the foregoing journeys, other reasons for being in the woods would call. These would include such pursuits as hunting morels, digging sassafras roots for tea, gathering hickory or other nuts, berrying, game spotting, or indeed, just hiking in the solitude of the peaceful environment. Many men and some lads also hunted roots of ginseng. The dried roots brought a handsome price. It took a lot of the root to weigh a pound, which was the unit of trade.

It would seem appropriate here to mention forest fires and methods of combating them. There were three or more wardens, each of whom had a regular crew. The wardens worked under an inspector, who was under jurisdiction of the State Department of Forests and Waters. Wardens were familiar with the terrain, trails, and access roads. Regular crew members were "minute men" who rated a higher hourly rate than recruits taken at random. I seem to recall a rate of forty cents, which would be paid from funds at the state capitol, usually many weeks after the fire. Each warden had equipment for his men. This included rakes with teeth like a mower blade, water spray tanks holding about five gallons, possibly being refilled from the nearest stream. One or two axes, mattocks, or shovels may be added.

From memory I estimate the number in a crew to be twelve. They needed to be in good physical condition as most fires were in mountainous territory, and often the work went on through the night. Wind conditions determined the direction of the fire, and one technique of fire fighting was to go in advance of the fire and clear a break by raking leaves towards the fire and back-firing, so that when the "head" of the fire reached the break it would die out. This was not always a success as high winds gave the advantage to the fire.

Carrying five gallons of water up hill, in the dark, was no easy task but the spray would help douse small tongues of fire or sparks at the break. After so many hours of fighting, the wardens would send to the nearest store for food. The menu would consist of cold cuts, cheese, ring bologna, crackers, bread, butter, mustard, catsup, cans of baked beans, sardines, possibly soft drinks, and cookies or ginger snaps. Food varied according to the grocer's stock. He also would be paid in due time. If fires persisted for days, fresh crews would be brought in, sometimes from long distances.

During those days many men were idle; and unreasonable as it may seem, fires were sometimes deliberately set. I never knew of anyone being apprehended for having done so. In a year or two burnt acres provided new black berry growth and more easily reached browse for deer.

As was said of deer hunting, volumes have been written about forest fires by more qualified people. Hopefully, this will serve as a generalization for benefit of some to whom it is an entirely new subject.

CHAPTER 20

Games

Although a great deal has been written about chores, house-keeping, gardening, etc., there was some time for playing, so long as it didn't interfere with necessary tasks. The games varied according to the ages of the children involved.

Since I was the youngest, we will think about entertainment for small fry. We had few "store boughten" toys for obvious reasons. I recall having a pressed-out tin truck, all from one piece of tin. It was simply pressed into a rectangular-shape with stationary wheels protruding from the bottom. There was no stationary sand pile, but always loose soil where one could make roads, bridges, houses, and barns. It was likely a prize in a rare "Cracker Jack" box. None-the-less, it furnished a lot of play time and lasted for months.

I remember a small two-wheel cart with about five inch diameter wheels, a low-box bed, and a two foot tongue. An old auto horn was nailed to a board which fit the bottom of the box and was aimed out the rear for a cannon. On July 4th we may have a few "penny stinker" fire crackers which came in a pack of ten. Frank, being two years my senior, generally fired the cannon. As we got larger we used a tomato can which came with a replaceable lid. A nail hole was made in the bottom of the can. A couple of grains of carbide were put in the can, sprinkled with water, and covered with the lid. Shortly, one would place a foot on the horizontal can and hold a match to the nail hole, blowing off the lid with a bang.

With an old wheel from a baby buggy and a three foot piece

of stiff wire, a "vehicle" could be made. The wire would be put through the axle hole and bent over. The other end of the wire would be bent into a sort of handle. This was used for many miles of running, while the driver made noise like an auto exhaust by blowing through lips or jaws. If a steel buggy tire was available, it could be run with shorter piece of stiff wire which was bent to form a "U" shaped "guider," with a handle eighteen or more inches long. These were good for much longer trips.

As the size of the boy increased, more sophisticated instruments were made. Sling shots were made from a "Y" shaped branch, onto the two tines of which were tied two strips of rubber cut from an old inner tube. On the other ends of the straps a rectangular piece of soft leather was tied. Into this, a marble size pebble could be slung at a considerable distance. It took much practice to control the point of impact of the pebble.

In the late summer, one could go to a crab apple thicket and sling crab apples. They were never really in short supply and time passed quickly. A sling was made with a long slender, flexible branch, the top of which was pointed. The crab apple was speared onto the point snugly. When the thrower swung a rapid, wide semi-circle, the apple would fly for rods. Of course, these apples would be widely scattered and unless found and eaten by a deer, mouse, rabbit, or some other wild creature, would sow crab apple trees where they were not necessarily needed or wanted. At this stage, no boy was aware of creating problems.

Another summertime game was caddy. An inch square strip of wood about four inches long was pointed on both ends. On one side was cut an X, and on successive sides, 1, 11, and 111. This was thrown from a distance into a ring scratched on the ground. If an X came up, the player lost his turn. If 11 came up, it meant he got two licks with a three foot long paddle. He would hit the end of the caddy, and when it flew up in the air, would strike it as hard as possible. Where it landed he would go and take his second strike. From its landing place he would measure off with the length of his foot the number of steps back to the circle, where the next player would take his turn. When all turns were taken, the one with the greatest distance won the round, or they could tally the distances for an established number of rounds and award the game to the highest number.

In winter a popular game was "shinny," known in other circles as field hockey. It was primarily a boys' game and each player supplied his own "club." This was a small tree branch, three to four feet long, with a piece of the root on the end at an angle. It resembled a golf club. An improvised goal would be set up on each end of the court. A wooden cube of about one inch was the puck. The name shinny doubtless was derived from the part of the anatomy which suffered the most abuse. It could, of course, be played on the ice with skates, but the only lake was quite a jog away and ice was not always sufficiently thick to be safe.

A fall evening game was a sort of team-hiding sport played after dark. A captain would take his team away from the base and hide them as best as he could. If he could circle and return from a different direction, it added deception. As the searching team ranged out hunting, the opposing captain would shout "Lay low sheep, watch the moon." When the searchers got far enough from base that the opposing captain felt one of his runners could reach base first, he would shout "skip." Whereupon, all players dashed for base. The team whose single player reached base first was the winner, and consequently became the hiding team.

For some time Frank and I shared a wagon, which I seemed to recall was called an "Overland." The rear axle was a steel rod thicker than a pencil. Near each end, a hole was bored where a bolt attached it to the wooden frame. These holes weakened the axle, which broke at somewhat regular intervals. Somehow, we would manage to get it to town where an older brother, Ford, had an auto repair shop. He fixed it repeatedly and sent it back. After so many of these episodes, Ford grew weary with the process and delivered a brand new "Simons Coaster" from the hardware store. Boy, what a windfall, with the name on each side in red letters! It also had solid metal wheels, unlike the wood spokes on the old wagon, and metal tires like spring wagons had. It had roller bearings, which we regularly cleaned and greased. We washed it, and after several summers, varnished it to its "like new" appearance. It was stored in a low cellar which was under the house addition where Dad's wheelbarrow was stored and kindling was neatly stacked. It was never exposed to the elements. When we finally outgrew the wagon stage, it was given to a nephew.

In winter, we coasted on any available slope in field or orchard, and since there was very little auto traffic, especially in winter, we rode on a secondary road not far from home. Once when I was still a preschooler, my brother Glenn, who was ten years my senior, took me sledding. We each had a sled which was too small for us, but we "made do." After some time Glenn decided it was time to go home. On the way, he traded ropes with me, and I was pulling the larger sled. He offered to trade with me, and it was local custom in cases of a swap to recite a short verse which ended "never trade back." I was elated!

Indoor social games were played by anyone inclined to join. We were allowed playing cards, Flinch, Old Maid, Dominoes, Checkers, etc. Some may read, sew, study, work puzzles, or read a story to small fry. We had a pump organ and would gather around it and sing. Some sisters played by ear and were more familiar with hymns, but other well known numbers were common. This would take place in the living room in a rather subdued noise level, as Dad might be in the kitchen reading the news and Mom doing crossword puzzles, or reading a novel, or Sunday School lesson. Sometimes one of them would be visiting, attending a meeting, or for Dad, loafing at the shoe shop.

Dad and I shared a birthday in January, and the traditional celebration was to have a taffy pull. Guests would come, including a bachelor cousin who, being his own cook, also had a formula for the taffy. He would cook the mixture and when finished, would ladle it out to each person on a greased pie pan or dish. When it cooled, it could be picked up in clean, greased hands and stretched and doubled repeatedly and, after a L-O-N-G time, would begin to harden. Impatient kids would sometimes take it out and lay it on clean snow, where it would harden quicker. Blisters were not uncommon. When it was too hard to pull, it would be coiled onto the pan or plate to harden even more. When finished it could be broken into small pieces by rapping it with a knife handle. Each could claim the fruit of his or her own labor and guests would take it home wrapped in wax paper or a paper bag as there was no plastic!

Occasionally, some family would have a play party for the older children. At these they would play "The Farmer Takes a Wife," adaptations of the Virginia Reel, spin the pan or bottle, ten little indians, blind man's bluff, and singing games. A light lunch might be served, as well as popcorn and hickory nuts for cracking. Always a kissing game or two, and maybe a riddle game would come into play. Swains would try to walk their favorite lasses home, usually in company of other couples.

As these young folks grew older, they, and usually some young married couples would attend square dances. Music would be provided by a combination of guitars, banjo, fiddle, harmonica, and the voice of the caller, who had to have learned a series of calls directing the actions of the dancers. Many romances blossomed at these functions.

Another favorite of young adults was Box Socials, usually held in the schoolhouse. A lady would pack a box which she decorated with crepe paper, dried flowers, cloth, or ornamental figures. The box would be filled with an elaborate lunch. The finished product was usually carried to the auctioneer's table by a third party so that the owner would be unknown. Couples who were going steady would employ devious means in order that the boyfriend could recognize his girlfriend's offering. Sometimes the bidding would thwart these attempts and the wrong bidder got to eat lunch and enjoy the lady's company. The inference that he would escort her home was not always honored. In any event, the charity for which the social was held received the proceeds. Entertainment of some sort was also usually furnished.

Outdoor picnics, sledding parties, skating parties, and hay rides were also popular with mixed groups. Men occasionally had chicken roasts at bonfires. Depending on what groups sponsored the affair, the source of the chickens was not always known to all. It took a long evening to kill, scald, clean, cut up, and cook the chickens. The broth was usually thickened with crackers, and each participant apparently furnished his own dish and spoon. There were no dishes to be washed en masse. The cooking pot and ladle must have been borrowed, as there was no coherent body, and participants changed from time-to-time.

Sometimes friends from elsewhere would attend these affairs, but as a general rule, these folks were all local.

CHAPTER 21

Occupations

It would, perhaps, have been better to write about occupations without reference to members of my family. It is also true that there should be no speculations about details of which one may not be certain. Therefore, writings relating to matters of which there was first hand knowledge seemed more prudent. I beg your indulgence for more family history in order to avoid alluding to something uncertain. Furthermore, it occurs that there may be some curiosity as to the outcome of the lives of this particular family of depression kids.

You have read earlier about Mrs. Rhem's store which had been in business for a long period. Her family had all grown up and she was up in her later years. The items shown earlier were sold in 1920. The store shown opposite had been in business before, but was acquired by A.C. Kinsey sometime in the later part of the decade. Had anyone known that the depression would continue, and become even more severe, it is hard to conjecture what course would have been taken by anyone! Be that as it may, the store did exist and was operated by my oldest brother, Al, shown in the accompanying photo.

Althought the wire overhead indicates that there was electricity by that time, the gasoline pumps were operated by the handle on which he has his hand. The back and forth movement of the handle forced the gas up into the glass container. The overflow in the glass container could be raised or lowered to measure by the gallon, from one to five. The hose was placed in the auto tank, and the gas released. The hose was carefully drained to as-

Brother Alfred at his store.

sure that the customer received all for which he would pay. An attendant always pumped the gas. The pump handle was detachable to avoid self-service. A look at the disc atop the pump with a magnifying glass shows that the distributor was "Freedom Oil Co." It came from a Pennsylvania town of the same name.

Early in my high school days I worked in the store and recall the following incident. There was a lad in town who had acquired a Model "T" Ford which, apparently, his grandfather was past driving any longer. He called it the "comet," and someone dubbed him the "captain." He would "taxi" on a contributory basis. At times, the contribution was minimal, and one day he came in for a nickel's worth of gasoline. The price was twenty cents per gallon. He got a quart of gas, which probably lost money for the seller, just in evaporation. It perpetuated a local tradition. Later, during a flash flood the "captain" was taking sightseers too close to the creekbed where the road had been washed away. The erosion didn't show atop the water, and the comet went down for the last time. No loss of life was suffered— only local legend.

Note the benches on either side of the doorway. These were for benefit of the loafers who had nothing more important to do, as many were out of work. Later on, the space between the buildings contained a "lobby" where they could congregate and be out of the way in the store. Ladies were reluctant to endure the scrutiny of many masculine eyes, and as a result many children came with shopping lists, and most of the buying was on credit. Each customer had a carbon copy pad of slips in the file. The second copy went with the order. Once a little girl came without a list and wanted to buy candy. She was asked, under suspicion, if she had money to which she replied, "Can't you get it on the flip?"

Notice the number of soft drink signs. It was a highly competitive market. Note also in the window the cluster of little American flags which flew from the hoods of cars, and were clamped around the radiator ornament. Enlargement of a sign in the left window shows "Three cakes of Palmolive soap for 29c, and one cake free." Just inside the door to the left was the candy case with a variety of one cent goodies. On the wall and shelf behind were varieties of tobacco products. "Wings" cigarettes sold for ten cents per pack of twenty. To accommodate smokers who had only pennies, an open pack was kept (likely illegally), and cigarettes were sold at two for one cent. For "rolling your own," a small package of Bugler, or 1860 tobacco and papers for rolling was sold for a nickel.

The room was heated by a coal stove. It also had a large ice box which held milk in quart and pint glass bottles, creamery butter, cheese, cold cuts, wieners, and bologna. Fleischman's yeast was wrapped in inch square packages, and many loafers habitually ate it, presumably for health. Longhorn cheese, which came in foot long rolls of six inch diameter and wrapped in waxed cheese cloth, was a favorite. Loafers often snacked on a dime's worth of cheese and a couple of soda crackers. Every couple of days the ice man would come and cut manageable size cakes of ice, which he carried, wrapped in burlap. This was for the refrigeration. When it melted, it dripped through a tube to the ground beneath the building.

If newly married couples could be located, they were always serenaded (also called "shivaree" in some localities). After much noise from a variety of sources, such as cow bells, pots and pans, bugles, and shotguns, the man selected as captain would call for quiet while he knocked on the door asking for the bride and groom. If insufficient noise had been made, more would be requested. Eventually, the couple came to the open door whereupon individuals came and offered congratulations and good wishes. When this was ended, the captain would call for more serenading, and the groom would fork over a sum of money. The finale was tendered, and the assemblage made way to the store to pass single file and be counted. The captain and grocer determined the per capita value to be given to each serenader. This, of course, depended on the number of people and generosity of the groom. The norm was probably ten to fifteen cents per person. The selection of the "bounty" was left to each individual and was usually carried away in a small paper bag.

As stated, most of the trade was done on a credit basis, the hope being that on pay day the total would be paid. This was not always the case, and some individuals always left a balance—the principal trap into which purveyors fell. When the business was sold late in the depression, this merchant found himself with about $10,000 on the books, some of which would later be paid. Some, regrettably, would never be paid, leaving him to liquidate his indebtedness with the fruit of his own labor. This he did in the course of years in order to protect his own integrity. To the everlasting credit of the heirs, one estate made restitution after the debtor's demise.

During this time another brother, Ford, was operating an auto repair shop in Ligonier, four miles away. This at a time when a lubrication and oil change cost $1.25, which price included having the windshield washed, the interior swept out, and air in the tires checked. He would occasionally go into Pittsburgh and purchase used Model "T's", make repairs on them, and resell them. He operated in an old building which had previously been a funeral parlor and furniture store—a typical combination of the day. It had three levels from rear to front with ramps joining the

Brother Ford at his auto repair shop.

levels. These were days of stiff competition and service was always prompt. If an employee were working in the rear when the bell rang, indicating a gas customer at the pump, he dropped the tool in hand and was enroute before it hit the floor.

Both of these operators were in various stages of building and operating summer cottages for seasonal vacationers. They could often have a debtor work off his debt with his labor—a sort of adaptation of burying a dead horse.

A third brother, Glenn, though everyone called him "Shupe," was later to be in the masonry contracting business. He built block foundations, stone walls, and chimneys; quarried and laid walk stone; and refurbished older structures. He was also a popular auctioneer and later elected township supervisor.

It was in these enterprises that my first awareness of the workings of the outside world emerged. During school vacation, some time could be spent in gaining work experience and earning an appropriate wage. In the later part of that decade my next older brother, Frank, and I went to high school. For at least two of the five winters covered, we were the only students from the village who traveled the four miles by whatever means we could

Auctioneer Brother Glenn at Compass Inn.

manage—much of it on foot. On completion of high school, we both enrolled at St. Vincent College as "day dodgers," fifteen miles away.

Frank went on to medical school and earned his M.D. degree, after which he specialized in roentgenology. He became Chief of X-ray at the Lewistown, Pennsylvania Hospital, a position he held for many years. To his everlasting credit, during his practicing years he established a checking account for Mom into which he made regualr deposits. She had never handled much of the family's finances, and anyway, she would have spent any money she had on someone else.

I later studied a course in hotel management, and became a manager four years prior to my entry into the military during World War II. Before retirement, I was Postmaster for ten years at Ligonier.

The oldest of the girls was Margaret, who to me was a sister who lived away from home and came regularly bearing gifts for all, but particularly for small fry. She worked for a lady who ran a boarding house while going to normal school, where she got a certificate to teach school. She taught for two or three terms before marrying Earl Bates, a veteran of W.W. I. Earl died in 1946 leaving her a widow with one teenage child at home. She returned to teaching on a temporary certificate, for by that time permanent teachers were required to have college degrees. As a grandmother she drove summers and weekends to a college forty miles distant, earning her degree while teaching. She then taught until retirement. Her early experience was in a one room school. She was extremely active in the local historical society and spearheaded a drive to establish a family museum. A book could, and should, be written about her contributions to church, family, and community.

The next girl in line agewise was Myrtle, who married Samuel Bills and spent her married life in devotion to her family. She equipped her two children for satisfying careers. She was an inveterate reader, as well as an able poetess who made contributions to the poetry society. Numerous poems of hers were published there, and by the Fort Ligonier Poetry Society. She was always generous to her younger siblings and was a wonderful companion at every age.

Estella followed next on the family tree of girls. She was seven years my senior, and in a large family, at the right age to become my second mother. Stories were always told of her having carried me around on her hip while Mom attended to other family needs. This would account for the cherished affinity we have always enjoyed. As of this writing in 1994, we two are the only surviving members of the family. She was always a spirited person who would undertake a solution to any problem, or see any project as a challenge. She was always lean, sprightly, and endowed with a great degree of energy. On the coming anniversary she and George Thomas will have been married seventy years. What seems like the happiest of those years were when they jointly were overseers of a country estate, from which employment they retired. They were active, devout, generous members of the church throughout their marriage.

Jean was next younger in the family, and of her short life you have already read.

Anna was the youngest of the girls, being only five years older than I. Naturally, we spent the longest time together and shared many experiences. She was the most musically accomplished of the family and furnished piano background for many singing sessions, both in and out of church. She was married to Robert Corter, who deserted her before their daughter was born. Five years later, she married Joseph West, a widower. During those years she worked at various minimum wage endeavors. I shall never forget that, out of her meager earnings, she bought for me the suit in which I graduated from high school. This was a measure of her generosity and love. The period was also an indication of her resolution and buoyancy of spirit.

During the five year period her daughter, Josie, became a blessed addition to our family. Though my parents never confided a concern to me, if what is written about the subject is true, the "empty nest" syndrome is a nostalgic reality. A dear and beautiful grandchild such as Josie added new spark to a somewhat bleak probability. I was a teenager whose ego was enhanced by a protégé who was inquisitive about the business of living. We formed a lasting and genial bond. Later in life she commented about the pleasant memories we shared. I was fortunate to have many nieces and nephews, all of whom were cherished. With no others, however, did I share the same household intimacy as with Josie.

Brother Frank—The Doctor

CHAPTER 22

Potpourri

One of the descriptions of potpourri is "a mixture, especially of unrelated objects, subjects, etc.," or "a collection of miscellaneous literary extracts." It is not certain how you would classify the following. Recently, someone wrote about classifications of things people accumulate. One of their categories was "no longer usable, but too good to throw away." Some of the following were recalled too late to list in the foregoing chapters, but it is hoped they may be of interest.

One of the residents of the village, seeing chicken feathers scattered on his yard, confirmed his suspicions that some chickens might have been stolen. He thought they might have gone to the home of a man who lived across the street. He went to visit the suspect and found him fast asleep having imbibed too heavily in some sort of spirits. Still warm, on the coal stove, was a pot of chicken parts which had been stewed. Returning from a trip back home with a box of epsom salts, he sprinkled a more than generous amount in the broth. A positive statement about the results cannot be made, but one of the rules of story telling is that something needs be left to the imagination of the listener or reader.

We were taught not to take much stock in superstition. As a boy I thought to try out one in secret, knowing that if it failed no one would be the wiser. I had heard that a wart could be removed by rubbing a stolen bacon skin over it, afterward burying the skin under the roof drips. As it deteriorated, the wart was supposed to disappear. As time went on the incident was forgotten, but, months later, I felt the knee where the wart had been. It was gone?!?

When I was large enough to carry newspapers, I sold the *Pittsburgh Press* for three cents per copy for the daily paper, and twenty-five cents for the Sunday issue. A lady customer taught me how to count change and gave generously of sage advice on other matters. She had a liking for toads, as she knew they would control insects on her flowers. She offered me a nickel for each toad delivered. It would be impossible to say how many were handed over, but of a certainty, her garden had more toads than any other flower garden in town. She had only one child; therefore, her husband's income could provide more of the finer things than most families had. They had a Willys-Knight Sedan, and I can still recall the radiator cap which held the knight with spear at port arms.

At one time there was a distillery where whiskey was stored. It was located in a brick building under which there was a crawl space. It was located on West Main Street in Ligonier, near the spot where Agway now is located. The building also once housed the highway department equipment shed. After its demolition, the Farm Bureau built on the site. The story is told that a group of men once entered the crawl space with auger and buckets. Having bored up through the first floor until they struck an upright barrel of whiskey, they bored through its head, and caught the draining spirits in the buckets. I could not authenticate this tale, but it makes an interesting story.

One of my older working brothers, who was still at home, bought a new bicycle on credit. While he as at work one day, the next younger brother rode the bicycle up the smooth grade of the highway. Shifting down again, he misjudged his speed and as he tried to negotiate the corner onto our road, he ran up the steps of Mrs. Rehm's store. The front wheel was bent beyond repair. Imagine the embarrassment of appearing before the seller of the bike and going further in debt for a new wheel! It was, of course, paid, and the brothers became friends again.

Once, a member of the family appropriated something which

belonged to an aunt. The deed was somehow discovered and, of course, punishment was in order. It was not satisfactory that the goods be stealthily returned to the rightful owner. The perpetrator was required to face the owner, confess to have taken something belonging to someone else, express regret, and promise never to repeat the deed. The light fingered tendency was thus abolished. The lesson must have been learned by all, as long after I was to learn of a similar situation a generation later, wherein the same successful procedure was employed. Indeed, there is ample evidence that many of the lessons of our parents have shown up in successive generations—"unto children's children."

Trick or treat was not practiced in those days. My recollections of Halloween as a small fry are largely associated with art work and ghost stories in school, along with drawings of fall scenery and practices. The lower teen years, however, have more memories of the annoying nuisances we must have made of ourselves in the neighborhood. The principal habit was that of throwing shelled corn against the window panes, creating a sudden racket indoors. This was done at a safe distance.

There were a couple of endeavors which had to be done at a closer and more daring range. A tick-tack was an arrangement whereby a thread was attached to a thumb tack in a window sash. By rubbing the thread with a piece of rosin, a screeching sound was made inside the pane. The origin and direction of the sound was not readily detected, and a few series could be made without detection. A more annoying noise could be made on a pane by a thread spool, through which a spike was placed and the circumference of which was notched. A string was knotted onto the spool and wrapped several times around it. By placing the notches on the spool against the window pane and jerking the string rapidly, a raucous noise resulted. This was usually good for only one jerk.

By this time, many gardens had cabbage roots from which the heads had been cut. These were excellent missiles for throwing against closed doors. Leftover tomatoes in a garden could also be thrown. Such antics were annoying, but usually not otherwise damaging. Once, for some such behavior, my brother Frank was captured by a man who happened to be visiting his mother whose house was being assaulted. He was led home by the ear and presented to Dad. The only punishment for the conduct was being sent to an early bedtime. Just in case of collusion on my part, I was sent to bed also. It is not to be supposed that members of the family were angelic. As seen, we had our weaknesses. There were, however, behavioral limits which we knew not to exceed.

The "big" boys in and out of the family, of whatever age, also had traditional treatments. One of these was to find two houses directly opposite each other on a narrow road. A light rope, probably binder twine, was tied to each door knob with a slight sag between. Both doors were knocked upon simultaneously. The system was not fool proof, but sometimes the person opening the door last received a jolt, or in any event a surprise. As mentioned elsewhere, back houses were upset. The really daring older boys have been known to take apart a farmer's buggy or spring wagon, and take it to the barn roof, piece by piece, and reassemble it.

For right or wrong, each community probably had its own adaptations of Halloween. Diversions were limited and some degree of innovation was likely inevitable.

Though All Fool's Day was not a holiday, it was a day long threat. Few did not get caught up in it at some time. I always admitted to being a slow starter and my better performances evolved in latter part of the day. Frank, on the other hand, woke alert and often trapped me with "April fool." I think on more than one occasion some remark about a robin was my downfall.

Christmas was always a delightful time. There was school vacation, but even in school there was related art work, compositions, songs, and anticipation. I don't recall any overall gift exchanges, probably because they were reserved for home and family. Very early there were no Christmas lights for lack of electricity. Enterprising folks may have green boughs and red ribbon on doors or windows. Cookies and homemade candies were favorites. Nuts and popcorn were not confined to Christmas, but were certainly in evidence. Ground pine could be found in many old fields which were reverting to natural state. This was used pre-Christmas for a small display on a stand with some small ornament or ribbon.

The tree would not be put up until December 24th. It would always be a hemlock tree, as they were native and grew in any size desired. They would not hold needles as long as pine or spruce, but they were abundant, especially in logged over tracts, most of which were owned by some firm or individual who was never to be seen, and who apparently had no objection. The mountain was common ground to the villagers.

The tree location was always in a corner of the living room. The old fashioned trimmings, many of which were cardboard religious scenes, were augmented by tinsel and strings of popcorn, some of which would be colored pink, probably with beet juice. Icicles and angel hair were non-existent. Small candles in holders could be placed on a table or stand, but were never allowed on the tree because of the risk of fire.

Some of the gifts for the small fry were offerings from the older siblings who were grown and generally married. These included some utilitarian items, and enough frivolous ones to make the hearts glad. Gifts exchanged by the home flock were generally some labor of love, requiring only time and talent.

Always the churches had religious plays, songs, cantatas, instrumental music, etc. It was important that the "reason for the season" was fully understood—a factor that has all but been eliminated in much current celebration. It is a sad commentary that the very entities who profit most from the tremendous upsurge of spending associated with Christmas, fail to emphasize the birth of Jesus Christ. Some Christians may also be guilty of this sorrowful neglect. For the Sunday School enrollees, there were treats consisting of such things as chocolate drops, hard tack candy, some English and hazel nuts, some chewing gum, and wonder of wonders—an orange!

It should be made clear that there was no garbage collection. There was little packaging requiring disposal. Any combustibles were burned. Regrettably, metal and glass were often dumped in some ravine. Plastic, as used in this day, was practically unknown. Many ecological problems are yet to be dealt with properly.

As a preschooler, I quite often had occasion to visit Mrs. Ankney who lived near by and had no children. We rather intrigued each other. Her house was always well kept and well furnished. She apparently had plenty of leisure to engage in this sort of social bartering. She told of things that were of interest to her. I may have furnished much of her knowledge about the workings of a youthful mind. In retrospect, it seems to have been mutually beneficial, as well as pleasant. I shall never forget that she taught me to whistle, an accomplishment from which I derived many hours of delight which lasted a lifetime.

By accident or design, I was often there at lunch time. While the fare varied, fresh eggs were often a part of it. Once when she asked how I like them cooked, I answered "over easy," which amused her no end. Our relationship has become a pleasant memory from childhood, and hopefully was a similar recollection for her.

The ages of either of us at the time is not now known, but my sister Estella and I shared a rare experience one bright summer day. She was at the age when it seemed it would be a wonderful experience to drive a Model "T" Ford. Our brother Shupe owned one and it was parked at home while he was out working. Estella's daring was matched by my enthusiasm to be a part of a ride. How the car was started is not recalled, but it probably had to be cranked, and she probably succeeded in cranking it. We started out on the dirt road leading away from the highway. As we approached the crest of the first hill, she began thinking of where to turn it around. Over the crest she decided to turn at the Welshonce lane, but her decision came too late to negotiate a ninety degree turn, and she ran into the fence post to the left of the lane. The impact threw me against and through the plate glass windshield, scraping my skull bone dangerously close to the left eye and causing liberal bleeding. At the first house on the return trek toward home, a lady gave us cloths to contain the bleeding and an old hat to keep off the hot sun. The Ford was left hugging hard against the leaning fence post. Dad was not apprised of the incident, and I was careful to expose only the good side of my head to him. Certainly, Shupe had recovery damage to overcome, but the relationship between he and the driver was not permanently damaged. Some other siblings and friends suggested that the permanent damage was to my head?! I have managed to live with it.

Varied Verse

Wool-Gathering

When it's time for mediation
   Or old-fashioned relaxation,
Find a quiet pillowed berth
   On the breast of Mother Earth.
Let the crowd's commotion cease.
   Hide your mind in favored peace.
Watch a soaring silent hawk.
   Hear a distant meadowlark.
Let concerns be vanished now.
   Wipe away the wrinkled brow.
Gather wool for comfort's shroud
   From a fleecy, floating cloud.

W.K. 1/93

Debtor

"Give me no more" my conscience wails,
   I stagger from the plenteous spread,
My soul is heavy with regret.
   I'm debtor still for daily bread.
But, should thy store be laden yet
   With gems thy heart is wont to give;
May I, though undeserving, taste
   Sweet gratitude for that I have.

W.K. '70-'80

A.B.C.'S

A woodland walk,
A dewy morn,
A prayerful talk,
A fine day born.

Birds a-wing,
Breezes tender,
Blessings bring,
Blahs surrender.

Chorus avian,
Chords a-blending,
Concert sylvan,
Concord sending.

On a distant branch a songster sits
and chops the morning into bits.

W.K. 2/93

Recompense

Weary from toil in field and wood
I laid my gift at heaven's door
And found, upon returning home,
My gift ten-fold—and even more!

W.K. '73-'74

Spring Magic

Nature gave us daffodils
That spring up in the cold.
One of her unexpected thrills,
To dare a stroke so bold.

From a ball in chilly earth
A bit of sun will lead
A greenish stem to sally forth
And conjure up a bud.

A yellow flash from whence?
With scalloped saucer holding.
A cup of splendid redolence
With lips of jagged moulding.

And even though it tilts aside,
Its contents never spills,
But wafts into a circle wide
While the beholder thrills.

W.K. 3/93

Masked Load

When any one we happen to encounter,
Most people speak of common, trivial things.
With friends we even may engage in banter,
But, pausing, other subject matter brings.
And, soon or late we talk about our trouble,
As though our burden only did exist;
But theirs, alas, the depth of pain may double,
And show our problem in a different twist.
Let's be aware the one we meet tomorrow,
Is fraught with care, regardless of a smile,
And may be laden with excess of sorrow,
That makes our load seem trivial the while.

W.K. 2/93

Green Pastures

The psalmist's pastures green
Were radiant beauty
Yet nature ruled that
Autumn's ruthless chill
Should steal away
The pigment, leaving bleakness
So, with the Spring
They'd all be greener still.

W.K. 2/15/45

Vicissitudes

Some folks strain for distant scene
    That may a new horizon make,
Restless, they, for pastures green
    Some want change for change's sake.

But others, on a sheltered course,
    Like creatures in their cozy lairs,
Feel they may be doing worse
    If life an unknown season bears.

By leaving the familiar haunts
    And treading in a different sphere,
Where, being, could affect the wants,
    And cause the calm to disappear.

No matter the desires we know,
    On which the fates of future hinge,
Nor how we wish the status quo,
    The simple certainty is change!

W.K. 3/93

Choose Ye

We see so much of evil brought
   In ordinary living
Rather than of goodness wrought
   .Our fellows to be giving.

No recent mode of action, this,
    Since time of Cain and Abel
But, the higher joys we miss
    By shunning conduct noble.

Must we ally with the devil
    Going up and down the earth,
Propagating plans for evil
    And opposing things of worth?

W.K. 3/93

Why Not?

We could
Do good
In measure great
If we
Could see
And meditate
On ways
To praise
Another's gain
And spill
Good will
To fellow man.

W.K. 3/93

Travelogue

We saw the beauty of the land
Unfold before our eyes,
A canyon in appearance grand
And wrapped in cloudless skies.

And in the spectrum, many a tone,
As through a magic lens,
Refraction spewing hues unknown
To our internal screens.

From angle, shadow, shaft of sun
   A differing sense ensued,
And left us, as it had begun
   In an ecstatic mood.

And then, to desert, lake, and nook
   — Where mountain ranges run
Snow capped in the distant look
   And pinkish in the sun.

Giant trees and pygmy roses,
   And geysers spitting steam,
Farther, icy water flows
   — A piscatorial dream!

Fields of grain, sand dunes bare,
   Crags to hillsides clinging,
Church spires shooting to the air,
   Crows and eagles winging.

Valleys nursing hamlets cozy,
   Wonderous sights at every bend.
Tribes of natives, cities busy
   — Suddenly, the journey ends.

Armchair version of creation,
   Loveliness for which all search,
But, the seats of grand sensation,
   — Rockers on our special porch.

W.K. 2/93

Reality

From a germ evolves a being
Starting with an inner urge
From a place of naught, yet growing
Giving forth the needed surge.

Nature has the tools for springing
Into life its useful trends,
Time and energy are twining
To create their helpful strands.

Health and strength the base for working,
Will and vision add the drive,
Planning, hoping, wanting, needing,
Make the fruitful time arrive.

Mixed are failures—fortunes beaming
Good and evil, lows and highs
Ever changing, flowing, streaming
Times with discipline and prize.

Take the joys and hurts in measure.
Ease sometimes gives way to strife
Mingling days of pain and pleasure
God ordained that this is life.

W.K. 1/93

Christmas Tree

Angel, holding highest sway
   Sing your song to us today,
Telling unto us is born
   To our world this yuletide morn,
He, the Son of God sublime
   Who speaks to us in every time,
Not alone to shepherds bold
   Tending flocks out in the cold,
But to those of this yule year,
   With heavy hearts of doubt and fear,
That gifts of peace can yet be had
   By looking to this Lamb of God.

W.K. 12/92

Fall Delight

Down, down, down....
    Suddenly a change of direction.
Then again—down, down,
    Like bits of paper strewn....
From a third story window.
    — Or a lacy feather from the wing
of a migrating bird.
    Would to God....
I could bring to someone
    As much enjoyment,
As is brought to me by
    ...Snowflakes!

W.K. '34

Renewal

It seems there is a lag in public spirit,
    Nor is it popular to wave the flag
No matter where we go, we always hear it,
    Especially we loathe the costly tag.

So, rightfully, we need to set about
    To check this demon in our common house.
This profligate needs to be weeded out,
    Lest we, too late, may suffer for our loss.

But we have asked too much of commonweal
    To win for us the goals we should attain,
And from ourselves we even try to steal
    Like puppies chase their tails and get no gain.

The moral fiber seems to need repair,
    Our forebears saw a future grand and bright,
Our conduct shows propensity to err
    God help us to arise and set it right.

And then with pride the flag will be unfurled.
    With all its scars and warts, our nation stands
Because there is no better in this world,
    If we will lend again our hearts and hands.

W.K. 4/93

Christ Is Born

Oh, what joyous hope we see
  In the beauteous Christmas tree!
Memories of childhood home,
  Assurances for years to come,
A kaleidoscope of hue
  Like a rainbow's colors show.
As I scan its figure comely
  One small light is glowing warmly,
Shiny trinket, gently blown,
  Reflecting from the mid-day sun.
We may ourselves a mirror be
  And emulate the yuletide tree,
Helping someone catch the reason
  For their happy Christmas season.

W.K. 12/92

Aid

A good man's hope will never end
  If God will spare him one real friend,
To buttress him today, tomorrow
  In his times of mirth or sorrow.

W.K. 3/93

Goliaths

I saw a little sparrow hawk
    Perching near some crows.
He sprang and darted for them
    And, suddenly, they rose.
He plummeted toward them
    And, much to my surprise,
They made a hasty exit
    From a fellow half their size.

W.K. 2/93

Ode To Polly

I know a lady whose dislike for winter
    Is so intense, a most unusual thing,
That when the grip of it prepares to splinter
    She actually begins to *taste* the spring.

She's so delighted basking in the sunshine
    Her spirits rise to an excessive height.
She'd opt, of course, to have the rays continue,
    And even grace the middle of the night.

W.K. 3/93

Chameleon

We cannot claim to own,
　　It sets on grass-plot sod
But only here on loan,
　　A maple, owned by God.

In harvest time it's green,
　　Background a deeper hue
Of grasses, shrubs, and pine
　　Enhancing more the view

Autumn alters this
　　Slowly, dimming, mellow,
Metamorphosis,
　　To a gorgeous yellow.

Time for winter's trip,
　　Color shifts to tan
Leaves are losing grip
　　Floating in the rain

Yule-tide decor plain
　　Looks a crystal bright
Now a tree aglow
　　In the noel night

Gray outreaching limbs
　　Up to skyward scene
Trusting nature's aims,
　　Spring—assuring green.

W.K. 2/93

Variant

In moments weak, my faith in self is shattered
Then, like a powered pendelum I sway.
When suddenly the dormant zeal awakens,
Again, I'm monarch of what I survey!
And in the interim I envy stoics
Who take the gifts of fate within the stride.
On second thought, when I am in the midway,
No tick, no tock—my better self has died!

W.K. 6/17/45

Foresight

If there's trouble,
— Not to worry.
One great day
We'll be in glory.
W.K. 11/92

Motive

Virtue smiles on those who give
    To ease the way that others live,
Some valued thing or helping hand,
    Deep from the heart—a gesture grand.

While some give charity with grace,
    Just to get some closet space.
Or lad who stacks the widow's wood
    So he can eat her berries good.

A man who gives in public eye
    To reap some harvest, by and by.
Deeds that leave impressions strong
    We sometimes do for reasons wrong.

W.K. 3/93

The Return

Jesus came…
And left a plan.
By His word…
He'll come again.

W.K. '94

Shirking

May God forgive
The way I live
Among the throng
Of evil, wrong.
And simply linger,
Raise no finger
In defense
Of innocence,
Lacking fight
To make it right.

W.K. '91

Dew

Morning glories blue,
Bright impatiens, too.
Looking up to say,
Lovely summer day.

W.K. '91

Karen

Dear child, when fate decreed you should depart
　　And in the going, crush a father's heart.
When all the depths of darkness did explode
　　Their dreadful, bitterest bile upon the load,
For all the worth of life—hemlock for me!
　　To stay, to go, the choice was hard to see
But, the conductor yet called not my train
　　And so, however dull, I must remain.
A sort of limbo I had never sought
　　'Twas grevious to travel as I ought.
For thyself, 'twas needless I should grieve,
　　For *me* I cried, since you must take your leave.
The gall that lingered seemed unlike to go
　　And time bade it dissolve so very slow.
In course, I felt to see you as you are,
　　Which helped to bind the lagging, hurtful scar.
And in the years that past you came to me,
　　In ways, my laden soul was somewhat free,
I'd conjure up your spirit in some bird
　　Who sweetly gave a song that could be heard.
Or, in a velvet petal I could feel
　　Or hear a melody whose balm did heal.
You doubtless joined your mother in the bliss
　　That God would give no greater joy than this,
And I should heed the holy writ, so born,
　　And live to meet with you upon the morn.

W.K. 5/93

Olden Orchard

A sunny morning in the early May
　　Where apple blossoms scatter down today
Where from the gnarled, aged, splintered trees
　　The feel of spring comes in a gentle breeze.

And fallen limbs lay scattered in the way
　　In grass where last year's shriveled apples lay
Yellow dandelion blooms abound,
　　Sweet myrrh and purple violets hug the ground.

One stands entranced, in wonder of the spell
　　And searches after even one morel,
But nothing robs the grandeur of the hour,
　　'Tis spring! and naught diminishes its power.

W.K. 5/93

Duped

'Tis true we mortals often err.
It seems a common trait.
But other creatures also share
And seek attractive bait.

A humming bird, clad green
Leaves lilac blooms aside
For more engaging scene,
— A red can of insecticide.

W.K. 6/93

Utter Recompense

In answer to a public need
A man's endeavor may succeed
And he receive an accolade
For the contribution made
As benefits to him accrue
Allowing for a status new
But, utmost joy will not attend
'Till he tells it to a friend.

W.K. 3/93

Champing

Lassies in their make-believe
Don old clothes from bygone days.
Longing for the adult years,
Imitating grownup ways.

Laddies also strive for growth,
Wearing Dad's old army tan,
Acting gestures of the aged,
Restless to grow into men.

Adults, too, the seasons rush
Wasting life in anxious plot,
Skipping over worthwhile joys,
Strive to get to where they're not.

W.K. 3/93

Ladies Aid

The Giver freely dealt
In varied measure full
From His abundant lot
Ample good for all.

Man, He gave an aide
Who lent a loving hand
To master what God made
And occupy the land.

From immemorial time
The mates have been a boon
In fashioning a home
Man could not do alone.

They lovingly enfold
Surrounding kin with care,
A family, young and old
The ministrations share.

Of all the blessings here
For humans in this life
To which so few compare
— A dear, devoted wife!

W.K. 2/93

Aspiration

This morning in the woods I sat
    Contemplating many a thing
And felt a lengthy tête-à-tête
    Of winter arguing with spring.

The breeze was neither warm nor chill
    And sky was dullish-bright.
It would be difficult to tell
    Which arguer was right.

And so, thought ran to other vein,
    Wandering to and fro
Nature's workings could be seen
    — Marvelous ways we'd like to know.

A dainty vine to skyward groped
    Twining 'round a giant tree,
I saw a parallel and hoped
    This "sprout" would cling to Thee!

W.K. 3/93

Cheerful Arias

What melodious mornings
Woodland springtimes make.
Birds from every quarter
Cause the sound to break.

Though they must be busy
Nesting for their broods.
Dangers may be lurking
While they search for foods.

Predators are roving
Always, in their world.
Stealthily they're moving
Catching what they could.

Accidents are common,
To creatures too they fall.
Unexpected tragedy
May be the lot of all.

But the birds, not planning
For ill-fated day
Go about their duties
Singing *anyway*.

W.K. 4/93

Wakeful

Father, what have I done this day
That steals away my peace of mind?
"Thrice shame upon thee, son of mine.
Thou hast forgotten to be kind."

W.K. '75 – '80

Promise

If we're faithful
While we're living
And our Master,
Always giving
Length of days
To offer service,
Promises
To ever love us.

W.K. 11/92

Composure

We are told not to borrow
A trial from tomorrow,
Lest doubly we pay
With the load of today.

But I climb ahead still
Before reaching the hill,
By evening I've tired
Undone, the aspired.

Why cannot I learn
To take in its turn
Each daily demand
As the Maker has planned?

Not gulping life down
Like gluttonous hound,
But nibbling like rabbits
With unhurried habits.

W.K. 4/93

Comfort

A good friend's care
For you will double
When you will share
With him your trouble.

W.K. 3/93

Toilers

I watch a team of workers,
Oblivious to all but task.
Their ceaseless effort seems a joy
And from the world, nothing ask.

Except, perhaps, for strength to serve
And instinct for the methods best,
Are grateful for an ample store,
Seem willingly to do the rest.

Some humans surely could take note,
Look on a duty with a zest
Like busy mates of Phoebes
Care for fledglings in their nest.

W.K. 6/93

Entreaty

Father, make of my life
    A conduit, through which trickles
Even the least drop,
    Of the milk of human kindness,
Springing from the fountain of your love.

W.K. 7/93

Renovation

Feel moist and pungent breath of after-storm
  When all must see the future now re-form.
Come, dawdle in a gentle tardy rain
  With lifted face erase some pampered pain,
Or walk among the various autumn leaves
  And feel secure with sight of harvest sheaves.
Take from a trusted friend the solace shared
  And feel the surge of hope from one who cared.
New strength of soul and courage now enfold
  Look forward to the new—blot out the old.

W.K.

Pie Dough

Sing a song of six bits
A pocket full of change,
Four and twenty pay days
You've tried to rearrange.

Payments on the mortgage,
Insurance, car and such
And now the cussed income tax
—it couldn't be that much!

And when the file is opened
Deductions disappear
Now isn't this a ghastly way
To start a brand new year?

W.K. '70

Inflation

Tinkle, tinkle, little dime
How your worth has changed in time.
Once you bought a milkshake—tall
Now you buy a coffee—small!

W.K. '40

The Auto

A wonderful rig is the auto,
   It gets you to there when ya' gotta
In comfort and ease
   And controlable breeze,
Tho it gives you a pain in the butta.

W.K. '89

A Bus

A bus is a clever machine
   It moves as you take in the scene,
For minimum money,
   With folks who are funny
It takes you from where you have been.

W.K. '89

Parody

Once upon a morning cheery,
   While I staggered, wan and bleary
From my quiet secluded lair
   After many an hour
Of sweet and blissful dreams.
   While I stumbled, nearly tripping,
Suddenly there came a dripping
   As of warmer water slipping,
Slipping from the tap in steam.
   "T'is your coffee," wifey muttered
"Coffee piping hot, with cream,
   Surely this will end your dream."

Ah!, how clearly stands the weakness,
   Forty years of morning sickness
And each separate rising fracas
   Wrought it's ghost across the day.
Eagerly I watched for evening,
   Since each morning found me grieving
For in surcease I am leaving—
   Leaving morpheus on his way,
For the mixed and dubious pleasure
   Of another hectic day,
Sagging spirit, pile of clay.

And the tough and sinewy thistle,
   Hid by lather, held by gristle
Sprung up, hung up with a gust
   'Gainst the battered razor's drag.
Then behind the water's splashing,
   There were visions past me flashing
Of the habit I'd be donning
   Made of blue misshapen rag
And accessories to match it.
   Binder twine around the bag,
Thus eliminating sag.

Presently my being quickened;
    Plotting for the day had thickened
Shoes were shined and gadgets gathered
    For the plying of the trade.
As I moved about the longer,
    Second coffee, smelling stronger
By degrees, the shades of azure
    Slowly their transition made.
The nocturnal anesthesia,
    Spiraling upward then would fade
Could be I would make the grade.

Deep into the daylight peering,
    From the threshold I stood leering
After breakfast, at the vast expanse
    Of world in ebb and flow
And I hopefully was yearning
    That a cure I would be learning
From the sages and their pages
    I must really come to know.
But my mirror from it's vantage,
    Struck a clean decisive blow—
Only I could make it so!

W.K. '50–'60

Night Sounds

Sometimes, during the little crannies
    Of wakefulness in the night, when you
Hear a dog bark in the distant, otherwise
    Quiet, one wishes that God would
Eradicate the fleas of its discomfort.
    Even as one wishes He would diminish
The little hurts in the lives of his
    Fellows—When, presently, the barking
Ceases and, in the quietness, both man
    And dog drift again into the blessed
Arms of sleep.

W.K. 7/93

Artisans

All builders we of something to remain
    With hope that labor's fruits be not in vain.
No matter what the fabrics we can weave
    Be they some worthy gifts our partings leave.
Let them be tones or words or helping hand,
    To ease the paths of some who tread behind.
Each builder has his own peculiar gift
    —An aid to some impending spirit's lift,
Some build or plan, as others crave to teach,
    But all aspire a blessed end to reach.
Lord, you have granted such ability
    But, cover us with grand humility.

W.K.

Refurbished

I spied a scarlet cardinal
    Sitting on a limb.
He had no way of knowing
    That I was watching him.

His yellow bill was busy
    Preening every tuft,
His stature seemed to double
    His garment was so puffed.

I felt a little guilty
    Spying on his bough,
And envied his dexterity
    When he succeeded so.

He was a nature study
    Perching in the sun,
It saddened me to see him go
    Whenever he was done.

I also thanked him silently
    For adding to my day,
But felt a twinge of emptiness
    As his beauty flowed away.

He likely sang again with pride
    As they are wont to do.
Having witnessed his renewal,
    My being lightened, too.

W.K. 8/94

Synopsis

There are nine requisites for contented living: health enough to make work a pleasure; wealth enough to support your needs; strength enough to battle with difficulties and overcome them; grace enough to confess your sins and forsake them; patience enough to toil until some good is accomplished; charity enough to see some good in your neighbors; love enough to move you to be useful and helpful to others; faith enough to make real the things of God; hope enough to remove all anxious fears concerning the future.

— Goethe

"Those who have little,
if they are good at managing,
must be counted among the rich."

Socrates 470-399 B.C.

The most significant things in life
cannot be bought or sold.

W.K.